MEDJUGORJE
A PILGRIM'S JOURNEY
A TRUE STORY OF SPIRITUAL GROWTH, CONVERSION, HEALING AND HOPE

Armando Minutoli

Published by
THE MORNING STAR PRESS
P.O. BOX 766
MEDFORD, NEW YORK, 11763

According to a decree of the Congregation for Doctrine of the Faith, approved by Pope Paul VI, (1966), it is permitted to publish, without an imprimatur, texts relating to new revelations, apparitions, prophecies or miracles. However, in accordance with the regulations of the Second Vatican Council, the publisher states that we do not wish to precede the judgement of the Church in this matter to which we humbly submit.

Scripture quotations in this publication are taken from the Holy Bible, New International Version, Copyright 1973, 1978, 1984, International Bible Society.

Photographs by:
Armando Minutoli and Adam Leskowicz

Cover design by:
Edward Barbini, EB Advertising, Islandia, N.Y.

MEDJUGORJE, A PILGRIM'S JOURNEY
Copyright © 1991 by The Morning Star Press. All rights reserved.
First printing
ISBN: 0-9630544-0-6
Library of Congress Catalog Card No: 91-75328
The Morning Star Press
P.O. Box 766
Medford, New York, 11763
(516) 732-5864

Contents

Preface i
Foreward iii
Introduction v
Prologue xi

PART ONE
1 - A Touch of Gold 1
2 - My Calling 5
3 - A Place of Messages 13
4 - Terms of Faith 33
5 - Our Celestial Visitor 37
6 - Cornelia 41
7 - Miracles are Forever 45
8 - Crisis and Healing 49
9 - Father Jozo 55
10 - The Local Flavor 59
11 - Gethsemane 63
12 - Journey to the Unknown 67
13 - Zagreb 71
14 - Traveling Home 81

PART TWO
15 - Return to Medjugorje 87
16 - Reminiscences and Miracles 91
17 - Krizevac and Healing 101
18 - Vicka and Marija 105
19 - Reunion - My Croation Family 113
20 - Slaying Dragons 123
21 - Happy Birthday Mary 129
22 - Feast of the Triumph of the Cross 133
23 - Matija, Marie, Miracles and Me 137
24 - Saying Goodbye 143
25 - Bridging Two Worlds 147
26 - Conclusion: The Onward Process of Conversion 155
Messages 167
Glossary 177
Other Resources 179

"I have come that they may have life, and have it to the full."

I Cor 2:12

To Our Blessed Mother,
the visionaries,
the loving people of Medjugorje,
and the Franciscan community
of St. James parish.

Acknowledgments

I would like to express my deep gratitude to my many friends for test reading this work, motivating me and providing me with constructive suggestions, criticisms, and prayers. Special mention must be made of author John Westermann and book editors Tony Bosnick and Jackie Eckert for their friendship, genuine enthusiasm, and professional assistance. Further acknowledement goes to Sylvia Rozakis for her generous motivation, advice and help in the first and second draft editing. Also, my special thanks goes to Bernie and Dotty Kennedy for making the production of the book possible.

Last but not least, my deepest expression of love for my wife, Joan, for her encouragement and patience with me during the writing process.

Through the writing period of this book the Lord has given me many blessings. I've made new friends, deepened relationship with existing friends and become the proud (young) grandfather of two grandsons, Justin Michael Batelli, born November 10, 1990 and Zachary Joseph Andrews, born March 31, 1991.

Preface

Mr. Armando Minutoli, a pilgrim to Medjugorje, is also a pilgrim in this book and in life as well. He is not a theologian, nor a person of fame, nor capable to influence the world with the might of his money. He is a pilgrim who speaks. A pilgrim is a man in search of something he knows he could become, but not without the help of God. Pilgrimage is the intimate experience of an individual, but also a common experience of man.

Armando is the name of the person who wrote this book, but to me this book is a voice of one pilgrim expressing the words of millions of those with a similar story of their own, who silently came and whose voice will not be heard and whose coming will not be recorded in the books of this world.

This book speaks about a human dream, about what a man would like to be, to know and to accomplish, and how to go about it. It is a story of this world, but please, never mind the story because it is not finished and will not be before arrival in heaven. This story is like a highway leading to the city of the final destination.

Here in this book a theologian might find words or sentences which theologically may not be precise, a writer might find sentences short of perfection, but everyone will find a witness of a dream, a search and a faith of Armando, a man traveling to the City of God, for whom Medjugorje was a place, a station of a meaningful rest to proceed further.

Father Svetosar Kraljevic, O.F.M.
St. James Parish, Medjugorje

Foreward

Since the publication of my first two crime novels, *High Crimes* and *Exit Wounds*, I have been asked on several occasions to help other fledgling writers with their manuscripts. I usually say yes because so many kind people helped me with mine. I read the work, make comments and corrections, send it back, wait. And nothing happens. Because more often than not what I have done is point out the need for a great deal more labor, the last thing most writers want to hear. Kurt Vonnegut once said that writing a book is like blowing up the Goodyear Blimp by mouth; anyone can do it. But not everyone is willing to do it.

That was not the case with the book you are holding in your hands.

No sooner was one section done than the next was waiting in my mailbox. I cut the hard-work portion of my advice and saved my breath. Here was a writer on a mission, who had made a level headed decision to tell a fantastic story to the widest possible audience, no matter the cost. Here was a man who heard a calling from the best part of his heart.

I told him it might take a year.
I told him it might not earn a dime.
He told me it was not at all about time or money.

It was about a world hurtling toward ecological and spiritual destruction, and the dire warning of our collective fate which is delivered to children nightly in the mountains of Yugoslavia by Our Blessed Mother. A message of terrible beauty. The message of Fatima. The message of Lourdes. The same as it ever was.

The world is not listening. Maybe not even the Church. But

one by one souls are waking up, and nudging other souls back in the direction of their faith. That's what's happened to me as a result of my involvement with this work; and very shortly thereafter I needed that faith, when my own mother passed away.

I remembered Al said at our first meeting, "If my story saves just one soul the torment of faithlessness..."

I think Al's story, Our Lady's story, actually, will do a whole lot more than that, and not a moment too soon.

Come to the mountain, Dear Reader. Your Mother is calling and the hour is late.

John Westermann
July 23, 1991

Introduction

This book began "writing itself" in my mind many years ago. I was approaching middle age and realizing that life's journey had an end. I'd always believed my mother had a preoccupation with death. I can still hear her saying: "When I die you'll feel sorry for what you said to me, or for what you forgot to say to me! You're going to miss me! You'll see! No one could ever love you like your mother." She seemed to be reminding and preparing herself and me for the inevitable. It doesn't matter how many scenes we play, or how many hit shows we have. All we can keep is our reputation. How we treat one another and the love we share that's what remains real and lasts. Love is eternal.

So, I asked myself, "What have you done so far?" In attempting to answer that question I carefully reviewed my life's accomplishments. I realized that whatever I had done or accumulated really had no lasting value. Certainly I was grateful for the plentiful life God had given me. However, I recognized I couldn't take anything with me.

Evangelist Billy Graham once asked the question, "Did you ever see a hearse pulling a u-haul-it with the man's worldly possessions?" Yet we seem to live our lives as if that's what happens. And what happens to all the wisdom we accumulate? The question echoes in my mind, "Is this all there is? You work, struggle and fight your entire life to educate yourself, to feed your family, and to build a society that you ultimately leave!"

Thomas Hart reminds us in his book, "To Know and Follow Jesus", of what Jesus taught on the simplicity of life:

> *Jesus tells us not to lay up treasure for ourselves on earth (Mt 6). He insists that we*

> *cannot serve God and mammon (Mt 6). He calls the poor blessed, and pronounces woes on the rich (Lk 6). In a paradigmatic encounter, He tells a rich young man that he should sell all he has and follow Him (Mk 10).*
>
> *He says that it is easier for a camel to get through the eye of a needle than for a rich person to enter God's kingdom (Mk 10). In a parable He depicts a man who is busy building himself bigger barns, and calls him a fool (Lk 16). His parable of the rich man and poor Lazarus puts Larzarus in the bosom of Abraham and the rich man in Hades (Lk 16).*

Hart goes on to say:

> *These are not Jesus' best loved teachings in the West today, where Christians enjoy affluence. It is hard to know how to live them. But it is impossible to deny or minimize them, given their frequency in the Gospels.*

Because of my childhood the search for success has been a driving force in my life. I was born unexpectedly, to immigrant parents at a late age. An only sister, twelve years my senior, was given the responsibility for rearing me and for managing the household. Both my parents worked in the garment industry sweat shops struggling to support the family, struggling to become part of a new society. They were subject to the devastating combination of immigration, the depression and World War II. Language was a barrier, along with prejudice and a background of emotional pain.

My mother had been abandoned by her father. She was then left in a convent school in Italy while her mother established a new life in America. My father's overbearing parents and the rejection of a childhood sweetheart drove him to the new land. As a merchant seamen he experienced being shipwrecked twice, both times being near death experiences. These two broken people met and clung to each other. They shared each other's need for permanence and legitimacy.

My arrival to the family was an additional burden for them. My mother had to work, leaving me to the care of my sister and babysitters. The separation caused by the necessity for my mother to work had a tremendous impact on me. My life was so restricted while growing up I was unable to develop a strong personal identity. As a child, I didn't have much self-esteem. I didn't believe my feelings were important. I had to be a prince and nothing less. Because of the disappointment she had with my grandfather and my father's erratic behavior, my mother needed a son to capture her image of the perfect male. The atmosphere in our home was always tense. We all had to live up to this quest for perfection; we had to have the best reputation, best clothes and best food — whatever the emotional cost! The pressure for my sister and me growing up was quite debilitating.

Many a Sunday or holiday dinner was interrupted with an argument that resulted in violent shouting matches. It was common practice for both my sister and me to throw up our meal almost as fast as we ate it. My hands had a tremor when I was eight years old. The love I received as a child was conditional on my behavior; you were good or bad, nothing in between. I grew up in a dysfunctional environment, therefore I wasn't able to develop the skills and gifts that God had given me. I realize now that my parents did the best they could and that there were many positive aspects to my upbringing. Yet it was hard for me to accept this fact until, over the course of many years, I had worked through my past and fought for my own identity.

In my effort to gain control of my destiny, I exhibited anger and was rebellious in school. My childhood relationships even suffered at times. The response I would get at home because of my actions was demeaning. Sometimes, kiddingly, they would call me the "black sheep" of the family.

I was called names like disgraceful, ungrateful, a jackal, undeserving and cream puff, which when said in Italian have an even deeper cutting effect. When I didn't follow the rules I was reminded that I was the "unexpected" arrival, which translated to me as "unwanted." In order to escape additional insults, I married at nineteen, seeking love and fulfillment from someone who also had come from an unhappy childhood background. The marriage lasted thirteen years.

In an effort to find personal fulfillment and gain acceptance I developed a success centered approach to life. I thought if I made a lot of money, I'd show them! For most of my career, my work has been in commission sales. This work appealed to me because it placed me in the limelight, along with giving me the potential for earning big money. My goal was to bring success to my family, a success that would identify me and mine as special and important. I needed to feel vital and needed. I was searching for something I had always yearned for; the affirmation and love of my family and friends.

Aggressively I plied my trade. What was important was to stay focused and get the job done. The end justified the means. My skill was to forcefully negotiate and influence decisions.

I was a self-proclaimed, contemporary gladiator fighting for the purse and a name. A person who would be respected. Someone with power and influence.

I played many roles: the sharp real estate broker, the politician with a cause—and more recently the executive headhunter, with the motto, "I always get my man." But never was I content, because somewhere inside I knew that it was all a game, knowing all too well that the final inning would have to be played.

Rich or poor, it was leading my family and me nowhere. I found myself lost in a desert of bitter loneliness. Distracted by the things that money can buy, I wandered aimlessly from one project or relationship to another, trying to satisfy a need for permanence beyond human scope.

Now I know that if I hadn't risked my worldly security and allowed myself this desert-like experience by journeying to the dark recesses of my soul, I never would have found my true identity and inheritance. It was only by accepting my vulnerability and fully admitting to myself that life is not mine to control, that I could allow God's grace to touch me. He waits patiently for us, waiting to welcome us all into His kingdom to take our royal places as His sons and daughters. What mortal father can offer his children eternal peace and happiness? (Mt 25:34).

If it hadn't been for a period of illness, the process of seeking my God might not have begun. Unfortunately, it seems that for most of us it's only in times of trouble, when we feel the weight of powerlessness, that we search for things that transcend our humanity.

Some of us use the same rule of thumb in searching for our God as we did searching for power and control. We visit mystics, follow gurus or allow the subtlety of evil to distract us from the real prize — God's unconditional love.

The plain and simple truth is that no gimmick or crystal ball, nor any action on our own part could ever compare to God's freely given gift of life and divine grace, which He bestows upon us each and every day!

For me the next question was, "If I were to die today, where am I going?" My only answer was to reach out to God. Although I was a Catholic who had received all the sacraments and participated in Church ceremonies and rituals, I didn't have a personal relationship with God. I didn't know God. Kidding myself all those years, rationalizing a relationship, I hadn't allowed God to enter my life. I felt the need to know God. I needed to know if there was a heaven, and could I get in?

My initial step was to read about the lives of saints; specifically the life of Francis of Assisi. Francis gave up enormous wealth and position as a nobleman to live a God-centered life. I found that the saints were devoted to Scripture. They ministered to others, just as Jesus did, and in poverty and humility modeled their lives after His example.

Following the lead of the saints, I began to minister to my brothers and sisters, and my world began to change. Scripture became real for me and I started to view things differently. As I progressed on my faith journey, I began to die to a world that has no lasting effect, a world that promises everything, but gives nothing. I felt I had just been been born into a world of hope and everlasting love. A world of forever beginnings with no endings—a world of wonder.

Medjugorje is God's gift to modern mankind. It comes in a time that is troubled by the destructive side effects of human progress and technology. It finds a world of atheistic communism, and sometimes selfish capitalism, along with rampant terrorism. A world that ignores the cry of the poor, a place where the voices of the sick and homeless go unheard. As you read my account, I ask you to be open. Look past what you read with your eyes. Let yourself feel the wonder of Our Blessed Lady's presence. Allow her to touch your heart.

She came to remind us that God does exist and that He loves us unconditionally. He's asking us through Our Lady to change our lives and turn to Him.

Medjugorje took away any doubt that I may have had about God and His existence. It gave me true affirmation of who I am and how much I am loved. It showed me how close God is to all of us, and how ready and willing He is to intervene on our behalf.

I now know that His grace has always been present in my life. Yet it was my own choice whether to accept Him or not. Walk with me on this pilgrimage. I know in my heart that the graces are not for me alone.

Prologue

Many books and articles have been written about the phenomena of Medjugorje, in addition to film documentaries and television news stories. Many of these give an accurate account of the history and facts surrounding the events that have taken place in the last ten years.

For those readers who are experiencing Medjugorje for the first time through this writing, I offer this brief overview, highlighting some of the major events. However, it is my sincere hope that the reader will be encouraged to seek out more information about this wonderful gift to humanity. This book is my personal account of the journey I have taken in search of my God. It is my hope to inspire those who read it to seek their own spiritual healing and conversion. A section at the end of this book lists some of the current reading and audio-visual materials available on the subject.

Medjugorje is located in the Croation Catholic region of Hercegovina in Yugoslavia. It is situated in a valley about eighty miles inland from the medieval city of Dubrovnik, which sits serenely on the Adriatic Sea.

This small village is inhabited by about five hundred Croation Catholic families, who form a farming community. They grow grapes for wine, wheat, and tobacco, and tend sheep.

The people of this hamlet are extremely hardworking and God-fearing. They have always maintained a deep faith in the Lord, accepting the burden of their toils in obedience to His will. Without the distractions of modern times, they live a simple, yet special life.

I believe it was because of their simplicity of heart that Our

Blessed Mother chose Medjugorje to make Her presence known here on earth. It is a place without material riches, but one rich in faith. On June 24, 1981, Our Lady appeared for the first time to six young children on a hill called Podbrdo, a rocky place with little vegetation, today known as "Apparition Hill" to the millions of pilgrims who have visited there.

Initially, the children were not believed. The skeptics included their families and friends, as well as the local parish priests. The children experienced the hardship of ridicule and disbelief. To date, the local bishop still remains skeptical, and at times makes things difficult for the visionaries and the parish's Franciscan clerics.

Most of the children are now young adults. Many of them continue to witness apparitions and converse with Our Lady each night. Their names are: Mirjana Dragicević, born on March 18, 1965, Ivanka Ivanković, born on April 21, 1966, Milka Pavlović, born on January 3, 1968, Vicka Ivanković, born on July 3, 1964, Ivan Dragicević, born on May 5, 1965, Jackov Čolo, born on June 3, 1971, and Marija Pavlović, born on April 1, 1965. There are two other young girls who hear and converse with Our Lady internally, but who have not seen her. Jelena Vasilj, born May 14, 1972 and Marijana Vasilj (no relation), born October 5, 1971, referred to as inner locutionists, have been experiencing this phenomena for the last seven years.

The apparitions have taken place in many different locations over the years, mostly due to the government's earlier suspicions. The communist authorities were of the opinion that there was an underlying political reason attached to these events. It was thought that possibly the children were being manipulated by activists.

More recently, the government authorities seem to have reversed their approach and are encouraging the building of hotel facilities to accommodate the ever increasing number of pilgrims. Apparently they are prospering from the revenue pilgrimage brings. However, they continue to keep a watchful eye on the visionaries and parish priests. Prior to the building of the new accommodations, the local peasants welcomed international visitors into their own homes and humbly shared whatever food they could offer, never accepting money for their hospitality.

This particular geographical area has a history of war and disturbances caused by political unrest. Because of the area's background and the concern of the authorities over the possibility of opening old political wounds, the children needed the protection of the Church. They were given asylum by the local parish priest, Father Jozo Zovko, who was the pastor of the Church of St. James, which had a parish enrollment of about thirty-four hundred parishioners at that time.

Father Jozo is said to have heard the voice of God, instructing him to protect the children. He was later tried and convicted by the communists for allegedly speaking out against the state. He was sentenced to prison for three years. Many of the village families were also interrogated and intimidated by the communist regime.

It is rumored that Father Jozo witnesses apparitions himself. He and the other Franciscan priests have been faithfully supporting the visionaries and ministering to the many visiting pilgrims. They all report and explain the same messages of Our Blessed Mother, who they affectionately refer to as, "Gospa" (Our Lady)

Millions of people have visited Medjugorje since the visions began. There have been many accounts of miracles. Thousands of pilgrims have claimed to have witnessed supernatural phenomena, physical cures and emotional healing, along with inner conversion and increased faith in God.

Our Lady explained to the children that she came to tell the world that God exists, and is asking for reconciliation and peace among everyone. Referring to us as her children and calling us to peace, faith, prayer, and fasting, her messages also warn of

Satan's increased activity and the urgency of immediate conversion. A section in the book, provides selected messages from Our Lady.

Many "incidences of supernatural phenomena" have been reported. Individuals and large and small groups of people, have simultaneously, and from different locations, directions, and distances, seen signs in the sun, large fires burning atop Apparition Hill (with no physical evidence of burnt terrain) and spinning columns of light atop Mt. Križevac (where a huge concrete cross is located).

This book hopes to present a picture of Medjugorje as an ever-continuing journey through faith for me personally. If this story serves to encourage, support or inspire one other person, I will consider the book a success.

1

A Touch of Gold

A COUPLE OF years ago my best buddy, Bob Frudenberg, joined my wife and me for dinner one night. Bob was a deacon at that time. I asked him about a comment he had made during his homily about the gifts and signs God gives to us at the past Sunday's Mass. While he was addressing the congregation, he got very excited, he put his hand in his pocket and came up with his rosary beads. He lifted them high for everyone to see. He said that his rosary beads had turned gold in color!

I asked Bob to explain what he meant about his beads turning gold. He told my wife Joan and me that his rosary beads had turned gold overnight! When he showed them to us he related that friends of his had visited Medjugorje, Yugoslavia, a place where the Blessed Virgin Mary was reported to be appearing to young Croation children. He said that some people's rosaries and jewelry had turned gold as a sign or gift from Our Lady, as an expression of Jesus' love for us. As this was happening in Medjugorje, it was also being experienced by pilgrims throughout the world. Bob mentioned that he had caught a little flack from our pastor about exhibiting the beads at Mass. Father was worried about scandal. Rome has not given formal approval yet as to the authenticity of the apparitions and is still in the process of investigating.

My feelings about this phenomena were quite mixed. Thoughts were going through my head like, "Maybe they are tarnished," and, "Isn't that a wonderful gift! God is really out there, and He really cares about us!" I became envious. "Why had Bob's rosary turned gold and not mine?" Then I began to rationalize, "Maybe it's because Bob's a deacon. He's a holy person." After all, I was just starting out on this journey of conversion and had a lot to learn about God.

At the time, I was in the process of fervently seeking a closer relationship with Our Lord, tirelessly looking for Him in His people, books, religious events, and the liturgy. The golden rosary was yet another spark which ignited my heart even further with a burning desire to search for and find God.

A few months later, while attending a healing Mass and standing in line in church by the altar waiting to rest in the spirit for the first time, I spotted a friend of mine, Geri. Geri Huber and her husband, John, are part of the healing ministry's prayer team.

She came over to me when I waved to her. I told her that I was very nervous about having hands laid on me (1Cor 12:28). In fact, I was down right scared. If you've ever been to one of these Masses you would admit that it looks very odd at first. People appeared to be passing out or overcome as the priest or deacon laid hands on them. They were falling into the arms of others who were assigned the task of catching them. Geri reassured me that there was nothing to be concerned about. It was a beautiful experience. She advised me to relax and let go.

Trying to make a joke of my nervousness, I took out my rosaries and showed them to her. "Anyhow Geri, my rosaries aren't turning gold either." I knew that hers also had turned gold. She took them in her hands and looked at them carefully. All of a sudden I heard her say; "Oh yes they are, Al. Look at the ends of the links. They're turning. See here! Look, look see!" They were turning gold! I could see it myself and I was stunned. That evening, I also rested in the spirit. It was a night of close moments with Jesus and remains a very special memory for me.

This sign from Our Lady was exactly what I needed. I needed hope in my life. It seemed for the last couple of years I was besieged by one disaster after another, reaching a point of crisis, a kind of crossroad. I had to either accept that there was a God in heaven, and He was going to help me through life, or I was doomed to anxiety and hopelessness, sentenced to a life that had no real purpose and face the ultimate irrational reality of death.

Our Lady was telling me that God really did exist, and that He was the cure for everything that ailed me. For me it was a message of hope.

Starting to pray the rosary more faithfully each day, I constantly watched my beads, hoping that they would continue to turn gold. I was impatient. Yet they progressively did. It was a sign I really needed. I had faith, but emotionally I didn't feel worthy of God's love, and with all my troubles it was hard for me to understand that God was indeed interested in me.

It seemed that everything was going wrong, a presence of darkness had developed over my life. My dad was on his death bed, attached to life support apparatus. My business was in crisis; creditors were at my heels, threatening and calling me names. Many more mishaps followed in quick succession. It was all taking an emotional toll on me.

Very little support was given to me at this time. On many occasions outright criticism was the only response I received from my immediate family. My close friends were amazed at the frequency and intensity of the pain that was being inflicted on me. The result was severe loneliness and depression. A friend of mine, Ed Pellicano, is a practicing psychiatrist and I asked to see him to discuss what was happening in my life. I was certain he would find me certifiably distraught or disturbed.

However, I was taken by surprise! He assured me that what I was experiencing was real and that he saw no evidence of pathology. Still there was no rational explanation for all that was happening to me. Even he considered the course of events to be quite unusual. He explained. Any normal person would feel depressed by the relentless tide of events I was experiencing. Many people would have cracked under similar pressure. His prescription was: "Pray." He felt that perhaps prayer would be the proper remedy (Mk 9:29)! When so many things are out of control spiritual recourse is best.

The fact that my rosaries were turning gold added meaning to his prescription of prayer. I saw this as a sign that I needed to focus on prayer and bolster my faith in this unusually dark period. While holding them in my hand I looked at them quite often in those times. Sitting by my Dad's deathbed, in court rooms, while on the phone with creditors, and while reading assorted hate mail.

Little did I realize that those changing rosary beads were an external sign of a progressing internal change. I started to recognize that nothing in my life was in my control. For the first time, in desperation, I had to totally turn to God, trust Him and to accept His will. I began this journey with the prayer gift of the Holy Rosary. My soul knew that it was being ministered to by prayer, but my mind found it hard to believe. I still needed the physical embrace of humanity to consider myself affirmed and healed.

2

My Calling

OUR LADY HAD touched my life. I would never be the same! I prayed for help to grow, to get closer to Jesus and to come to terms with my fears and self-doubt. Also I prayed to experience God's love for me, to be affirmed; this was something that my family had been unable to do for me while I was growing up. Through prayer I began to grow spiritually, and growing is always painful. Yet my rosary was always at hand to bring Jesus's loving presence into my life.

My approach to ministry began to change. One afternoon I heard a fundamentalist preacher on the radio quote Mother Teresa as saying that God expects us to be "faithful, not necessarily successful." It reminded me of the importance of letting go, and letting God decide how He wanted to use me.

The faith sharing I was experiencing in my Cursillo community (see glossary) and group reunion was consistent with that concept. It finally started to sink in. However, letting go is not an easy task.

As time passed, the word "Medjugorje" kept coming up. Some friends in our community had visited there and were really touched by the whole experience. As others spoke about their pilgrimages and about what they have witnessed, a great interest was kindled within me. I began to read books and watch video tapes on the subject. The books I read always uplifted me. They were all fast reading, even for someone like me who normally agonizes through books.

On occasion I would talk about the apparitions to the young people we were ministering to, some of whom were suffering from the impact of substance abuse. Interest seemed to awaken in them. It gave them something to believe in, something that transcended what they considered to be their hopeless lives. The concept that someone could really love and accept them unconditionally was instilled in them.

It had the same effect on me. I began to fantasize about traveling to Medjugorje, but thought that would be impossible for me. You see, I was almost forty-four years old and had never even boarded an airplane. I had always had phobia problems, including fear of tight spaces and heights, among others. I would never survive a trip of that proportion. No way! Out of the question!

People in my community started talking about a new book about Medjugorje. They were impressed, marveling that a Lutheran had written it. The next time I visited my favorite religious book store, I spotted a display of the book and bought a copy. It was too exciting to put down! I felt the experience that the author Wayne Weibel was describing. It was real for me. Our Lady was touching me with each page I read.

Near the end of the book, toward the last ten to fifteen pages, I started to feel quite ecstatic. Out of nowhere an internal voice said to me:

> ***Armando (that's my birth name)... I want you to come, you'll have a couple of rough moments but it will be a growth experience for you.***

I started to doubt and question myself. Could it be possible that the Blessed Mother would speak to me? Yet at the same time I was experiencing a fullness inside. Feelings of peace and joy were overflowing in me. I felt I would burst.

Then I was really on fire! I grabbed my coat. I was already very late for my Tuesday night men's group, but I was anxious to share this experience with the guys. Just then, my wife came out of the bedroom. She had just woke from a nap.

"Joan! you'll never believe what just happened to me!" I cried. She said "Who was on the phone before?" "Joan! While I was reading the book about Medjugorje, Mother Mary spoke to me!" To this Joan responded, "Did you feed the dog?" "That's it, Joan! I'm going to my group. Goodbye!" (A prophet is never truly loved or understood in his own town! (Mt 13:57). The drive to the meeting was like riding on a magic carpet. "The guys would understand," I thought. And you know, they did! Even though the compelling feeling inside me was so difficult to relate. I was being called, but how could I answer? I couldn't pull this off! I can't fly!

It seemed we were all on fire that evening. Our Lady had touched the entire group. Somehow I spit out the words, "I would like to go, but I've never flown!" One of the guys, Pete Trupia and his wife, Diane, said they too were interested in making a pilgrimage.

She said, very assertively, that she would look into the arrangements and get the details for us. I was in trouble now! Diane Trupia was not the type that took "no" for an answer. A few days later, she called with the information and we were going! "You'll be alright! Flying is a piece of cake," she tried to reassure me.

Diane said she would inform more people in our Cursillo community and in her own parish. If we could get enough people together we could benefit from a group rate.

My heart wanted to go, but my mind told me that it was

impossible, I couldn't go through with it. Still I felt compelled to try and I acted as if I could! Diane planned the trip to coincide with school recess. That gave me three months to adjust and accept this venture, and honestly speaking, I had an underlying hope that it would all go away.

Praying night and day, part of me really wanted to go. I had felt drawn by Medjugorje for years now. Everything I heard about it enthralled me. The feeling was always with me.

Now I was beginning to tell friends and family about going, and encouraging them to join us, still only half believing that I could go.

The more people I told and asked for their prayers to help me accomplish this mission, the more determined I became to attempt it. It was almost as if this were a test for me. The more people who knew of my intentions, the more I'd have to face if I failed. How could someone who supposedly had a strong faith in God, not trust that he would be given the grace necessary to realize this calling? I was stuck now! I had exposed myself and felt trapped.

At times the pressure on me was quite heavy. It even caused me to have an anxiety attack in my shower, while just thinking about this endeavor. It was on my mind every day. It became an obsession! It was all I talked about! Asking people about their flight experiences, I tried to find reassurance for myself. A few weeks prior to my flight, the Avianca plane crash disaster occured on Long Island. A week later I read a blurb in the local newspaper stating that the U.S. State Department had posted a warning alert for possible terrorist action directed at U.S. travelers and American interests In Europe.

My friends did their best to convince me to go. "Al," they would say, "if Our Lady is calling, you have to go!" They prayed for me, fasted and encouraged me. They gave me books and subliminal relaxation tapes about overcoming air travel phobias. I began to feel that if I could just board the plane, Our Lady would take care of the rest.

I was packed at least three weeks in advance. My friend Ed had given me prescriptions for tranquilizers and sleeping pills in case I began to feel frenzied on the plane.

I read the phobia book cover to cover, twice. I played the relaxation tape so often that if I even heard the word 'relax' I would pass out. Inside me I began to feel some peace through the prayer of my friends.

Unconsciously, I even arranged a going away party for myself, using my wife's upcoming birthday as the reason. We prepared a celebration dinner, complete with a cake and a "Happy Birthday" song. We went through all the motions, but we knew in our hearts it was a bon voyage party. Everyone was concerned, knowing how tough it was going to be for me to board that plane. That last minute resassurance and support was something I so desperately needed.

Whether I realized it or not, I guess I wanted to see my entire family together before leaving in the event I didn't return. I found out later that the consensus was that I would not board the plane. They were afraid for me.

The day of the trip finally arrived. Pete and Diane picked me up and I was fine until I had to say goodbye to Joan. I was overcome by full-blown panic. I said to myself "I can't do this! I'm not going!" Diane told me later that she felt she had lost me at that moment. However, as I forced myself to get in the car, the anxiety immediately subsided.

The Lord was asking me to do very little on my own. "Put yourself into my hands! Just open the door a little, Al, and I'll flood you with My grace!"

The trip to the airport was comfortable. Diane and Pete made small talk. I could sense that they were waiting for the other shoe to drop.

After we arrived at the airport, we checked in and waited! I looked out the windows hoping to see planes taking off and landing. This was an exercise suggested in my air flight phobia book. The idea was if you could look at planes successfully accomplishing takeoffs and landings, you would be able to visualize the plane you were flying on as having the same success.

Until I reached my seat on the 747, I was perfectly calm. Then, from what Diane Trupia and Anne Cooke told me, I turned as white a ghost! A surge of anxiety hit me. I remembered what Anne's daughter had suggested if I became afraid! Pray to God and ask Him to take away anything between Him and me. The attack lasted a few seconds, the color returned to my face and I sat down and relaxed. This was my first miracle! My prayers and the prayers of my wonderful community of Christian friends had been realized!

My seat was next to the steward's service area. As we were getting ready to taxi, I told the flight attendant "This is my first flight." At the same time she spotted my rosary beads in my hand and immediately got an expression of panic on her face. Better her than me! I'm sure the thought running through her head was, "This guy must be crazy to take a long transatlantic flight for his first flying experience." She must have envisioned a trip of terror with someone going bonkers, scratching at the exit doors, somewhere over the Atlantic.

Not only was I flying, but I was relaxed and enjoying the trip! I ate, slept, looked out at the clouds and remembered what my spiritual director had said, "Think of the song lyric, 'I've looked at clouds from both sides now.' I felt like I was Neil Armstrong going to the moon. Jet engines give you a lift in many ways.

We had a swift six-and-a-half hour transatlantic flight and connected immediately at Frankfurt, Germany, with our flight to Zagreb, Yugoslavia. After a short wait, we continued our flight to Dubrovnik.

The airport at Dubrovnik is surrounded by mountains and there's a draft of wind which lends character to landings there. However, by this time I was already feeling like a seasoned flyer.

No sleeping pills for me. What self-respecting astronaut would take sleeping pills anyway?

We went through customs easily and boarded a van for our trip to Medjugorje. As the van climbed through rocky mountains, I noticed the countryside was different from what I had expected. Even with little vegetation, it was still quite beautiful.

Continuing along, we passed high above the walled city of Dubrovnik. How majestic it looked, nestled between mountains and the sea. Its medieval presence told me the people here had roots that were centuries old.

We were scheduled to spend a day visiting Dubrovnik on our return. This was arranged to insure that our flight connection would be made safely on time. However, the Lord had other plans for me. I was to visit a Dubrovnik, but not the one I expected.

3

A Place of Messages

WE ARRIVED IN MEDJUGORJE after dark and placed our bags in our rooms. The rooms were unexpectedly new, with private baths. We were all so very tired from our overnight travel without sleep. But we had made it! Praise Jesus! A miracle! Without unpacking, we proceeded directly to the church of St. James.

The evening Croation Mass had already concluded, however, we were in time for the Benediction. The people of the parish sang beautifully in their native tongue, obviously with much love in their hearts.

After services we walked back to our guest house and had dinner with the rest of our group. Anne, Diane, and I had arrived separate from the rest of the group as we had taken a different airline. We introduced ourselves to each other before retiring.

The next morning I awoke to a beautiful day! Looking through my shower window, I was surprised to see a big cross on top of the mountain where our house was nestled. It was Mt. Križevac, a very special and holy place. A place of signs and wonders that I had read and heard about. Being on that mountain was an honor for me. Little did I know then how I would never be able to forget what I would see through that window.

Going downstairs to the dining room for breakfast I met some of the other people in the group. Gail Yorkowitz, a fellow student in Pastoral Formation (see glossary) with me was there. We had been on a class retreat weekend together the previous fall. Then I saw another former classmate, Bob Campbell, from my Parish Outreach course. One of the insights that I was hoping to gain from this pilgrimage was to come to terms with a calling I felt for the diaconate. Was it a coincidence that Bob was a deacon and Gail was in formation classes with me (a prerequisite to the diaconate)? In the course of talking and sharing with Gail and Bob I began to think more about pursuing that vocation. Almost immediately, I started to receive affirmation for some of my feelings.

As I left for the 10 o'clock English Mass, I could see the church in the valley from our front door. The valley was so peaceful, with Alpine-like snow-covered mountains as its backdrop. The crow of a rooster reminded me of the videos I had seen about Medjugorje. I remembered the sounds I had heard in them.

The villagers greeted me, said hello and smiled. I stopped and greeted a peasant woman. She shook my hand, took notice of my rosary beads, lifted them to her lips and kissed them. We spontaneously hugged each other. I felt embraced by God. There's so much love in the people of Medjugorje, language is no barrier. There are very few distractions between them and God!

The pilgrims were invited to a talk in the church by Father Slavo, one of the spirit-filled Franciscans who has worked with the visionaries since the time of the first apparition. He has authored respected books on the subject. His talk was quite inspiring. He amplified Our Lady's messages of prayer and conversion by relating them to Gospel stories. Our Lady's love and warmth shone through his words.

After Father's talk we attended a Mass said in English. Bob Cambell assisted Father at Mass. For me, this was another close moment with Christ. To see Bob, a Long Island deacon, on the altar in this holy place overwhelmed me! Just to be in the same church that Our Lady visits, made me feel both honored and unworthy. After Mass, we all walked up the hill to Jelena Vasilj's home. She lived two houses away from my guest house.

Jelena is one of the two young girls who converse with Our Lady. The other girl is Marijana. Jelena and Marijana are called "inner locutionists." They hear Our Lady but do not see her. They have been experiencing this for the last seven years. Jelena was ten when Our Lady first communicated with her in February 1982.

Overtaken by Our Lady's appearances to the visionary children, Jelena and Marijana were moved to prayer, even to the extent of giving up their play time, which is a prime activity for most seven-year-old children. One day they heard Our Lady's voice and the internal apparitions have continued for them since that time. The Madonna appeared to them initially in a white dress. In one of her messages to Jelena the Blessed Mother said:

> *Dear children, I would like for the whole world to be my child, but it does not want it. I wish to give everything for the world, for that, Pray!*

At the end of that year, Jelena asked Our Lady if she too would receive the ten secrets that were revealed to the visionaries. the reply was:

> *I do not appear to you as to the other six because my plan is different. To them I entrusted messages and secrets. Forgive me if I cannot tell you the secrets which I have entrusted to them. This is a grace which is for them, but not for you. I appeared to you for the purpose of helping you to progress in spiritual life and*

> *through your intermediary I want to lead people to holiness.*

The visionaries were given ten secrets which they have not yet disclosed. The last secret was given to Mirjana on Christmas Day 1982.

The seers know the date when the secrets will be divulged. According to the visionaries a permanent sign will be left on Apparition Hill three days after the disclosure. It will be left there for those who do not believe. In early December 1982, Jelena received the following regarding the sign:

> *Hurry to be converted. Do not wait for the great sign. For the unbelievers, it will then be too late to be converted. For you who have the faith, this time constitutes a great opportunity for you to be converted, and to deepen your faith. Fast on bread and water before every feast, and prepare yourselves through prayer.*

Our Lady also gave them messages in April 1983, concerning the urgency of conversion. Early in the month, Our Lady in tears, said to Jelena:

> *I give all the graces to those who commit grave sins, but they do not convert. Pray! Pray for them! Do not wait for Friday. Pray now. Today your prayers and your penance are necessary to me.*

Later that month her message reiterated the urgency:

> *Be converted! it will be too late when the sign comes. Beforehand, several warnings will be given to the world. Hurry to be converted. I need your prayers and your penance.*
>
> *My heart is burning with love for you. For you it is enough to be converted. To ask questions*

unimportant. Be converted. Hurry, proclaim it. Tell everyone that it is my wish, and that I do not cease repeating it. Be converted. Be converted. It is not difficult for me to suffer for you. I beg you, be converted.

I will pray to my Son to spare you the punishment. Be converted without delay. You do not know the plans of God; you will not be able to know them. You will not know what God will send, nor what He will do. I ask you only to be converted. That is what I wish. Be converted! Be ready for everything, but, be converted. That is part of conversion. Goodbye, and may peace be with you.

In late May Our Lady asked Jelena and Marijana to recruit twenty young people to form a prayer group which Our Lady would supervise and give spiritual direction to, creating a model of community prayer for the whole world. In the middle of June she dictated the rules for the prayer group to Jelena as follows:

(1) *Renounce all passions and all inordinate desires. Avoid television, particularly evil programs, excessive sports, the unreasonable enjoyment of food and drink, alcohol, tobacco, etc.*

(2) *Abandon yourselves to God without restrictions.*

(3) *Definitely eliminate all anguish. Whoever abandons himself to God does not have room in his heart for anguish. Difficulties will persist, but they will serve for spiritual growth and will render Glory to God.*

(4) *Love your enemies. Banish from your heart,*

hatred, bitterness, preconceived judgments. Pray for your enemies and call the Divine Blessing over them.

(5) *Fast twice a week on bread and water. Join the group at least once a week.*

(6) *Devote at least three hours to prayer daily, of which at least is half an hour in the morning and half an hour in the evening. Holy Mass and the prayer of the rosary are included in this time of prayer. Set aside moments of prayer in the course of the day, and each time the circumstances permit it, receive Holy Communion. Pray with great meditation. Do not look at your watch all the time, but allow yourself to be led by the grace of God. Do not concern yourself with things of this world, but entrust all that in prayer to Our Heavenly Father. If one is very preoccupied, he will not be able to pray well because internal serenity is lacking. God will contribute to lead to a successful end the things of here below, if one strives to work for God's things.*

Those who attend school or go to work must pray half an hour in the morning and in the evening, and, if possible, participate in the Eucharist. It is necessary to extend the spirit of prayer to daily work, that is to say, to accompany work with prayer.

(7) *Be prudent because the devil tempts all those who have made a resolution to consecrate themselves to God, most particularly, those people. He will suggest to them that they are*

praying too much, they are fasting too much, that they must be like other young people and go in search of pleasures. Have them not listen to him, nor obey him. It is to the voice of the Blessed Mother that they should pay attention. When they will be strengthened in their faith, the devil will no longer be able to seduce them.

(8) Pray very much for the bishop and those who hold positions in the Church. No less than half of their prayers and sacrifices must be devoted to this intention.

Our Lady concluded her statement to Jelena that day with:

I have come to tell the world that God is truth; He exists. True happiness and the fullness of life are in Him. I have come here as Queen of Peace to tell the world that peace is necessary for the salvation of the world. In God, one finds true joy from which true peace is derived.

Jelena was a bright, sweet and unassuming teenager. Her sincerity and love for God were quite evident. She was very patient, full of peace and interested in answering all our questions, a characteristic that was later demonstrated by the visionaries.

The seers relate to others as family! Through them, I sensed that we were all connected. It reminded me of the scripture passage "We are many parts of one body" (1Cor 12:20).

After visiting with Jelena we returned to our house to freshen up. Bob invited me to lunch to chat and catch up on old times. On our way toward town to a restaurant he knew, Jelena and a friend passed us. She smiled warmly and waved, making me consciously aware for the first time in my life of how much I am a part of God and His family on earth.

During lunch Bob suggested that I spend time alone, pray, and be observant. I should allow Medjugorje to unfold for me, he suggested. Already, unbeknownst to himself, he affirmed something that I was experiencing. For some reason it was difficult bonding with the people in our group. Usually there is more of a closeness between pilgrims. It seemed that the people in our group were more interested in doing things independently, than in staying together and sharing the experience.

Bob and I had a great lunch together. I really needed to be with a friend and the Lord had provided one. Bob remarked that he found me to be more peaceful and with a greater acceptance of life, since he'd last seen me two years earlier. His observation made me happy because I had been working and praying hard to develop those strengths. In fact, my New Year's resolution had been to attain more "trust" in God. Taking the Medjugorje trip was a big step in that direction.

The sun was shining through the window and I glanced in its direction for a second or two. Looking back inside the darkened restaurant again, sun spots developed before my eyes. There's nothing unusual about sun spots. We've all experienced them. However, these sun spots were different. They were golden in color, each turning into the shape of a golden sweetheart. Finding this unusual, I turned my eyes back toward the sun again, as a test, and looked back into the darkened room. The same thing happened.

This all took place while I was speaking with Bob. Yet I discounted it. Maybe it was the deflection of the glass, an accidental occurrence of some kind, an optical illusion.

About two weeks later, after returning home, I rented the latest video on Medjugorje, one that I hadn't seen before. As I was watching, the narrator on Apparition Hill, looking out to the next mountain range, exclaimed that the people present including herself and the other narrator, were seeing little golden sweethearts emanating from the sun.

Realizing what I had experienced in the restaurant, I filled with joy, giving thanks to Our Lady! Tears started rolling down my cheeks. Our Lady had even thought to give me a welcome home present! I was elated, and just sat there in my den. Was this a coincidence? Here I was in the same room, sitting in the same chair as when I had heard that inner voice that first encouraged me to go to Medjugorje. This was a true miracle. Still the earthbound side of me did not allow it to register.

Sitting there my mind began to wonder about how many other miracles I had neglected to believe in. Drifting back in time, I remembered a crossroad in my life, a time of crisis, without the peace and serenity I now enjoy. A time when chasing stars was for other people not me. A lifestyle filled with drink, superficial relationships and loneliness. However, in hindsight I could see that even in that dark period there was always a twinkle of hope.

My real estate business fell apart because of the recession. So I closed up shop and secured a position as a banquet manager for a local catering house. My duties included officiating at weekday evening client parties and meetings. After closing one late Wednesday night, I decided to stop for a relaxing drink before going home. Entering the lounge of a hotel and catering complex I noticed a beautiful young woman serving behind the bar. She was exceptionally stunning. There was only one other customer, who was sitting at the other end of the bar writing in a note pad.

I ordered a drink and glanced over towards him, noticing that as he completed a page he tore it off and handed it to the barmaid. She half laughed as she read the paper, raising her eyebrows, then quickly placed it beside the register. This happened a few times in succession and after a while this fellow got up and went to the men's room.

The barmaid walked over to me and introduced herself as Maria. While making some small talk, she reached over to the cash register and picked up a wad of register receipts and showed them to me. She explained they were poems this fellow had written for her since the start of her shift. It was now two in the morning. She went on to explain that they left a lot to be desired, and apparently, many were in poor taste.

When he returned, he wrote her another and handed it to her. She read it quickly and handed it to me. The man wasn't too pleased, but I complimented him and Maria winked at me.

I asked Maria for a few napkins and began writing my own poems, as a spoof. But the drink, and the long day at work started getting to me. My defenses were down. Unexpectedly I wrote a poem that had a lot more emotion and feeling in it than I intended. But it didn't fit the moment. It just jumped out of me, and reading it again I couldn't believe that they were my words. Reluctantly I showed it to Maria who was touched by it. To my embarassment, she handed it to the other fellow. He read it, immediately paid his check and left in a huff. We laughed as he left. It was getting near closing time. Maria invited me back for Friday night. Complimenting me on my writing, she told me that I was a nice guy and she would introduce me to the regulars.

I went back that Friday and many other Fridays, Saturdays and Wednesdays. With Maria's initial coaxing, later followed by Richie the bartender, my newfound friend's, I became a regular. While consuming excessive amounts of straight imported vodka, I would write poems to the female patrons on cocktail napkins that Richie would generously supply. He would recommend willing subjects to me. Any gimmick to keep people interested in drinking. Richie was quite a salesman, my glass was never empty. I got to meet all the girls and they would spend time at the bar and order drinks.

It wasn't long before my interior motivations took over my conscious efforts. As much as I wanted to create flattering prose as a means of endearing myself to these woman, what I wrote had more than superficial impact on them. My writing hit areas deep inside their hearts. At times I could sense what was troubling them, almost automatically customizing my poems to their present state of life. Many times it appeared to give them the little hope they needed. Sometimes the poems would suggest a new course of action, others would affirm their feelings.

It got scary at times. The prose would seem to really hit home, it related to people's most intimate feelings. My poems revealed parts of their personal life they had never shared with anyone. Shocked and amazed they would look at me as if I was a mind-reader. At times their reactions gave me goose bumps. I became known as "the Poet of Apple Annie's." It amazed all of us. The regulars would literally protect me, making sure that there was a seat for me so I could write, running interference so I wouldn't be disturbed while writing. The women in our group would caution me about other women. Sometimes they intervened if they perceived someone to be insensitive or unworthy of my creativity.

I loved the attention. The men in our group initially asked me to write for their girlfriends. As time progressed they eventually asked me to write for them, including my ex-Marine friend Richie the bartender and our buddy Frank the cop. Both these guys were capable of being rough and tough, yet their gentleness would surface many a time with this poetry business. They couldn't wait to read the lastest release.

We had a community of sorts. People who really cared and looked out for one another. In our own way we were all shipwrecked and in transition, hoping for our lives to change. I believe to this day that the Lord gave us that interlude together. We cared for, supported, and encouraged one another.

Who would ever have thought that this expression of inner feeling would surface in a cocktail lounge? Over the months as I continued to write, my prose began to take on a spiritual tone:

> ***Follow your heart, journey afar to furthest of all faraway stars...Measure no distance of your spirit...Experience your life with adventurer's delight...Fear not the comets, and darkness of***

> night...For your vision the light of your travel, a pathway of hope in spiritual flight...No journey so taken could fail in its way...For your heart is with you, never far away...

It seemed that I had great insight into other people, but never acknowledged the significance of what I wrote for myself. Others had the right to hope, not me. I wasn't good enough, smart enough, etc. "There is a future!" I would shout in all that I wrote. However for me it was elusive.

I wrote about stars in those days, never thinking that they would ever touch me:

> Stars sparkle and glow...Although they are vast and majestic...Appear most beautiful as a speck in the sky...A divine simplicity...Talent and intellect, gifts of nature...Wholeness of heart and spirit, the truth of life and love...I see you Lady with that sparkle constant and bright...Journey no further from my sight...

As I look back, I can clearly see how Our Lord was working inside me. It was as if the spirit within was clambering to come out; I was just too distracted to notice. His infinite love was calling me out of the darkness, but I wasn't listening. I believe that writing about stars was no accident. I think my Medjugorje experience began a lot sooner than the actual trip. I wrote my poems around the same time that Our Lady began appearing in Medjugorje.

After lunch Bob and I went to the church to pray the Rosary and prepare for Our Lady's apparition. The priest led the prayers in Croation and the responses were in various languages, English, Italian, German, etc., yet it was harmonious. I knew inside myself that the only barriers we had between us were the ones we created ourselves. Here we were, all equally called and loved by Our Lady. She brought us together, embracing us and touching each of us a special way. She showed us how to love one another and how to enjoy each other's God-given gifts, implanting this message in us like a seed to grow in the world.

Walking back from church each night, the sky always seemed to be alive with shining stars and I would recall the events of my day, noticing how the presence of peace had taken hold in me.

We returned home for dinner, conversed for a short time in the dining room and then retired.

One night on the way to my room, I was invited by my traveling companions Diane and Anne to stop by the room they were sharing. While they showed me some wonderful religious articles they had purchased as gifts we shared some of the experiences of the day. We were all tired, so I said good night and proceeded to my room to prepare for bed. It has been my practice, over the years, when traveling and sleeping in a hotel to usually leave the light on in the bathroom. I did the same that night and slipped into my pajamas. Before getting into bed, something told me to look out the bathroom window up towards the cross, so I went back into the bathroom and turned off the light.

From my window I saw a very bright star in the same spot where the cross was atop the mountain. I said to myself: "Gee, isn't that beautiful!" The other stars in the heavens, also seemed to be brighter than normal. Some of these other stars were actually blinking on and off, like beacons.

While I continued to look at this massive star, it started to move. Was it an airplane? Then it proceeded to move up and down. It had to be a helicopter, but what would a helicopter be doing out here in this remote place, at this late hour?

The object began to descend and grow larger, taking the shape of a star — the kind teachers put on students' homework. It climbed straight up, then down, then side to side. It dawned on me that it was making the sign of the cross. I couldn't believe what I was witnessing. It was so spectacular! Words really cannot accurately describe it. I received a surge of joy, sensing within me that Our Lady was present in that star! What a wonderful gift! On one hand, it felt so natural and comfortable, however on the other, my rational side found it difficult to compute. It was like having the ability to communicate on a multidimensional level. We are so used to Hollywood's special effects that the vision itself was believable. However, this was not a Steven Spielberg production. This was literally and figuratively far above anything he could ever produce.

The message came through! God is out there and wants us to know Him, to be with Him, and to love Him! As I experienced this outward sign of love I praised Jesus and Our Lady. I have never stopped thanking them since.

Collecting myself, and realizing that this vision of love wasn't leaving very quickly, I ran down the hall and knocked on Diane and Anne's door. "There's something you must see! Come to my room quickly!" At the same time, I thought, "What if they don't see what I see!" They would probably think that I was experiencing a delayed psychotic episode from my flying phobia.

They followed me immediately and we all squeezed into my shower and looked up toward the summit of the mountain.

Thank God, they saw it too! I was relieved. In fact, they started to observe other things. Pointing them out to me! We noticed changes in color, a red halo around the star, with little red stars circling it.

The thought kept going through my mind, "Am I that special? Does God really love me so much, that he would strengthen my faith with this magnificent sign?" Oh how wonderful it must have been for the early disciples, to have experienced Our Lord's presence, walking side by side with Him on earth!

Little did I know that Our Lady's star was going to appear to us every evening. Some people suggested it could be seen between the hours of 9:30 pm and 11:30 pm. I didn't keep track of the exact time but when I looked up at Cross Mountain in the evening her star was there. I got the feeling that Our Lady was tucking us in. One night I watched her star return to space. It climbed ever so slowly into the heavens and then disappeared. The other stars dimmed and the sky above the mountain returned to its natural color. Everything about Our Lady is so gentle, and loving, including Her magnificent star!

In one of the liturgies I attended, the priest referred to Our Lady as the "Morning Star." It choked me to hear this in church. It really had meaning for me now. How many times in the past did I hear Our Lady being referred to as the "Morning Star" but never understood what it meant. I felt so happy and grateful for her presence and I continued to praise and thank Our Mother and Our Lord.

The next morning I woke up late, and after showering, bent down for something and got dizzy. It made me nervous. Thinking it was probably jet lag and that I should move slowly, I walked down to the dining room for breakfast, still a bit off balance. I began to feel better physically after eating some food, but emotionally I was still a little shaken. I didn't mention it to anyone hoping it would just go away.

Gail invited me to meet and visit with a Franciscan nun, Sister Francis Magdalen. Sister, a retired nurse, was part of our tour group. She had taken ill with the flu and was in her room recuperating. She turned out to be a wonderful, open and honest, spirit-filled person. We talked and prayed the Rosary together. This was another very close moment with Christ for me. The Lord's prescription for what ailed me was to do service to another. My dizziness disappeared.

The warm encounters we had together that week helped reconcile me with my parochial school past. My spiritual director at home had encouraged me to visit with some of the nuns who had taught me in school when I was a little boy, the ones who were at times abusive, leaving me with unhappy childhood memories. She felt that it would help in inner healing. The nuns who taught me were now probably around sister's senior age.

I was reluctant. What possible good would it serve to bring up these old hurts to aged nuns? I'm sure they did their best to serve God and his children. How could I disturb the hard earned retirement of these nuns? Sister and I were in the midst of prayer when Bob joined us. A short time later, Bob's roommate, Rich, a young seminarian also came in and prayed with us. There I was, only moments before feeling sorry for myself, dizzy, alone. Now I found myself in the company of three loving pilgrims in communal prayer and companionship. The message was becoming convincingly clearer to me, making me see that I wasn't alone. Asking me to trust and grow, the Lord was saying, "Al, recognize your faith in a practical relationship with me. I'm here with you! Whatever the circumstance. I'm involved. I care."

Another morning, Sister and I prayed the Rosary together. She shared such great insights and she gave me spiritual direction and affirmation. Her observations and suggestions were uncanny. She touched parts of my struggle that I had not even disclosed. Leaving Sister to prepare for her nap, I walked down to church. Mary Fistler, a young American woman was to give our orientation talk in the gazebo at the rear of the church.

Mary turned out to be quite dynamic and inspiring. She related her experience of conversion at Medjugorje, saying she was a confirmed atheist, who wound up visiting Medjugorje on a dare. After her initial experience there, she returned to the U.S. Nothing seemed to make her happy. Feeling called to serve Our Lord in Medjugorje, she left her home again, returning to work and witness to pilgrims. Mary has a wonderful depth of love and peace in her. You could tell that the Lord had intimately touched her heart.

When the orientation was finished I walked around the side of the church. People were gathering at the side door, around one of the visionaries, Vicka, as she was leaving the church. Pilgrims were shaking her hand and asking her questions. I started to take some pictures of her, but there were so many pilgrims and locals crowded around her that I didn't think my shots would come out. Then all of a sudden she was right in front of me, all by herself. I was so surprised I was unable to speak! We shook hands. I had seen her and the other visionaries on videos, many times, but never imagined that I would see any of them in person. My seeing her and shaking her hand was fortunate. Our group was scheduled to meet with her the next afternoon, but by then she had come down with a virus.

While visiting the church each day I saw an Italian priest, whom I recognized from the first video I had seen about Medjugorje. He prayed the Rosary each day and concelebrated Mass. One afternoon I approached him and introduced myself. His name was Father Pietro Zorza. He was an Italian missionary priest assigned to Glasgow, Scotland, of all places. Isn't it funny? I only thought of missionary activity in Third World countries. I explained to Father about the video and promised to send him a copy. He mentioned to me that he remembered giving a taped interview, but had never seen how it came out. Would he allow his picture to be taken with me? He enthusiastically set up the shot, mustering into service one of the Italian pilgrims standing nearby. Father Peter very carefully directed the shot, making sure that this kind fellow got us in the picture, with the choir loft window as a back drop (Our Lady appears to the children each evening in the choir loft). Father was a very warm man. Meeting him in person confirmed for me that I had fulfilled part of my destiny and the dream.

As I continued to observe all these people, it dawned on me that there are no superstars. We all have a common bond, our God. It occurred to me that when we truly believe in Him and His love for us, being the best and the most successful has no relevance. The patience and humility of the visionaries and the local priests, exemplify the strength and power of God's love and peace.

As events were unfolding, I began to notice more and more,

that Our Lady's gentle hand was in all my activities. Guiding me step by step, she was helping me see and grow, encouraging me to confront unresolved issues. Her presence was making me feel welcome. Introducing me to others who would have spiritual impact on me, she was bestowing on me many graces along the way. She was my tour guide! My Morning Star!

Deacon Bob invited me to participate in a Communion service he was going to conduct for Sister Francis Magdalen in her room after Mass, so I returned to my room to change and freshen up. A little while later, on my way to Sister's room, I heard singing in the dining room. As I passed the glass doors leading into the dining room, our host Jozo, invited me in.

There were about twelve men in the room, eating cookies, drinking coffee and wine, laughing, joking, telling stories, periodically singing Croation folk songs. Jozo explained that once a year he and his friends would take a mock hunting trip. The men of the village, along with their teenage sons, would go to the mountains searching for game. If they saw any animals they would shoot in the other direction. After these so called hunting trips they would end up in one of their companion's houses and celebrate together the trophies they didn't take.

The group made me feel welcome. They respect one another and are one with the environment, accepting their lives with resolve, and gratified by whatever the Lord bestows on them. God is a very big part of their journey. They even make covenants with Him in the Old Testament tradition "If we ring the church bell each day, Armando, the Lord responds with good weather for our vineyards and crops," remarked Jozo.

That invitation and that moment to relax and be affirmed was important to me. Our Lady wasn't missing a trick. Not knowing it at the time, I was going to need and trust Jozo later in the week.

Arriving a little late for Sister's prayer service, I explained that I had been "forced" to drink wine with the local hunters to celebrate their success. It was a tradition that couldn't be violated. I don't think my story was believed.

4

Terms of Faith

ONE MORNING WE BEGAN the trek up Apparition Hill (Podbro), the site where Our Lady first appeared to the children. I became nervous as we maneuvered through the steep rocky path. Suffering from vertigo because of an inner ear problem, I was having trouble keeping my balance at times. The higher I got, the more uncomfortable I became. When we finally got to the top, I clung to a rock trying to pray, while reprimanding myself for not having more faith. When our group eventually started down I was very relieved.

During the descent my steps became lighter and the negative thoughts about myself dwindled. Upon reaching the bottom of the hill I felt peaceful and resolved to try it again another time.

Ann and I decided to explore. We followed a road that appeared to be in the direction of our guest house. The weather was so pleasant: like a typical summer day the noon sun was shining brightly. We walked past a large bull with great big eyes, who was corralled in a stone pen in the front yard of a house. As we passed him he cried out loudly, apparently wanting our attention. We laughed and got the impression that he felt insulted and snubbed. When we walked up to him to say hello, his expressive eyes were saying: "What am I, chopped liver? I'm one of God's creatures too!"

As we continued along the road I remembered that someone said we would be visiting Vicka's house for an inteview and that it might be on this road. We were curious about how the visionaries lived, so we asked one of the passing peasants if she could point out the house for us. It turned out that we were directly across the street from it. The lady also told us in broken English: "That Vicka mother," pointing toward a couple on the front patio. As we looked over, Vicka's mother smiled at us and came closer to the gate to say hello. I felt as if we were imposing on them by being so interested in their private lives. It must be difficult for them at times. I'm sure they miss their privacy sometimes. Yet this kind of down-to-earth encounter showed me the real unity we have as God's children.

Later that day, I was encouraged to go to confession and was directed to an American priest. It took over an hour and a half of waiting on line to see him. I was told that he was thorough and took people's concerns very seriously. The priest wanted me to unburden myself of all the sins I had ever committed, even the ones of which I had already been absolved. This disturbed me, putting me in a state of shock, bringing me to the point of tears. I couldn't understand why The Lord would bring me to Medjugorje and give me the strength to overcome obstacles, allow me to witness miracles, only to be admonished for sins I had committed in my youth, sins that had been confessed and absolved many years before.

Falling into the old trap again, the "guilt and sin God" I had learned about in my childhood surfaced in my mind. Then I started to question Father's direction. Quoting scripture to him like the stories of the Pharisees and Sadducees. I asked him,

"Where's Jesus's love in all this?" I felt as if it were Father's opinion that evil and sin had more importance than God's love for His children. It was his conviction, that the slightest sin not confronted had a hold on our soul. I wondered whether this priest had a problem with the Church's post Vatican II interpretation of Catholic doctrine, specifically regarding the personal examination of conscience (the internal forum).

This incident was a paramount step for me in receiving a healing for the self-doubt I had experienced for many years. Here I was in this very holy place, a place full of special graces, a place of active communication from God and Our Mother. This was a place of apparitions and miracles! I found myself in the position of having to confront the conservative viewpoints of a devoted priest, while maintaining the courage of my faith in God, my convictions and those of my spiritual directors. In my view, God is not only a God of ritual and religion, but also God of relationships and a loving presence within each and every one of us. He is a God accessible and visible in the faith experience of His children. If I am to become closer to God, I need to differentiate between religion and experiences of faith. I believe that through receiving the Eucharist and developing a personal intimacy with my God through prayer, along with the faith sharing of other Christians, sin and evil will have no room in my life.

Many of us have become so accustomed to a formal church structure that we forget that we too are the church. We may have depended so strongly on the Church in the past that we may now be experiencing the same type of gap that sometime exists between parents and children. When we put religious on a pedestal, we isolate them.

We all have an individual responsibility to study scripture and to make decisions based on our faith. By not doing this we inhibit the formulation of our conscience, limiting our ability to identify the elements of good and evil in our lives. I know I must cooperate with the Church's teaching and accept God's graces for my redemption. However, the responsibility for choices is mine. The Church can guide me, educate me, and minister to my spiritual and sacramental need, but it's the process of my conversion (metanoia) which allows me to accept God into my life and heart, by adopting a faith-filled relationship with Him.

I was pretty down when I left the church that afternoon. Part of me wished that the encounter with Father never happened, but I knew deep inside that it was part of my journey and healing. I had to truly come to terms with who I am, and trust my convictions of faith and those of my spiritual Father at home in the States.

5

Our Celestial Visitor

MASS WAS UPLIFTING. The wonderful singing in Croation touched my heart. When I remember Medjugorje I can still hear that singing. God's presence is keenly felt in the loving voices of the devout villagers, who after working long hours in the fields all day, squeeze together patiently in an unheated church, to worship and adore their Savior each night. Many times they sacrifice their seats for pilgrims.

After Mass that evening we were to join the visionaries atop Apparition Hill in prayer and song while we waited for Our Lady to appear. While climbing the hill, I was not as relaxed and resolved as I had hoped to be. Fortunately I could walk up with Ann, who had a flashlight.

When we reached the top, Anne continued past the spot where we initially stopped, taking her flashlight with her. I was embarrassed to let her know my feelings. On the hill again, I was feeling dizzy and afraid without a flashlight of my own, unable to descend the steep rocky path if I wanted to and finding myself once more in a position where I had no choice, having to accept circumstances that were not in my control. That lonely, unworthy feeling began to rise in me once more. I resigned myself to prayer and tried not to think of my dilemma.

Then all of a sudden there was silence. I knew Our Lady had arrived, but I was unable to see the visionaries go into ecstasy from where I was positioned. It was very dark and many pilgrims were crowded around them. Immediately after the apparition, the visionaries led us in prayers of thanksgiving. Then they shared Our Lady's message. Her words were translated only seconds later. Right there on the spot, each word was deciphered and read to us in English. Her message that evening was:

> *Dear children, your mother wants to warn you tonight that satan is attacking very strongly at this time. Don't permit within yourself to have any emptiness. Close this emptiness with prayer... At this time the prayer is the medicine that will defend you against Satan in a spiritual way. Dear children, with prayer prepare yourself for lent.*

Mary gave us pilgrims our own special message that night through Ivan and Maria, the two visionaries who were present.

> *She prayed an Our Father and a Glory Be with us, blessed us and took our petitions to God. She also gave us homework. She asked us to "Pray the Glorious Mysteries of the Rosary when we return home" Then she said "Go in the peace of God my dear little children."*

After we heard the message, we started to descend the hill. I became very peaceful and exceptionally light on my feet. My descent was cushioned. All fear and discomfort left me. We were all very happy as we made our way home. Our Lady's message alerted me more keenly to the attacks of Satan and I began to see that some of the mishaps I was experiencing were inspired or cultivated by him.

The next day after Mass, I returned to our guest house and met Maria Cenatiempo, one of the other pilgrims in our group. She had traveled to Medjugorje with her two young children, Daniel and Melissa. I had spoken to her briefly here and there, but we hadn't had a conversation of any duration. She was very attentive and loving to her children.

Maria told me she had just returned from a walk with her daughter Melissa and that she had met two elderly villagers. The wife, she explained, was in need of aspirin for a toothache. She promised to return later and bring them the medication. Maria asked me to accompany her back to meet the villagers. She said she would take me to a very special spot she found, to pray the Rosary. I hesitated a moment then accepted her invitation. She shared with me that while she prayed there earlier that morning, she was filled inside with a tremendous sense of Our Lady's presence. She noticed a large flock of tiny birds, nestled in the bushes close by, singing happily and loudly.

We met after lunch and started for the villager's house. As we strolled, I commented that I was very glad she had invited me, expressing to her some of my feelings about disconnection from the group. She said she had felt the same way. We focused on the possible causes. It occurred to us simultaneously that the antimagnetism we were experiencing, might be the Lord's way of calling us to a more prayerful and intimate relationship with Him. Things finally started to fall into place. We couldn't talk to Our Lord if we were preoccupied with other conversations or distractions. We realized what a gift He had given us in one another.

As we approached the village couple's home, we heard the husband, who was sitting out front, call to his wife, who seemed to be cooking inside. As she came out of the small, aged building I noticed that she had a handkerchief tied around her chin to soothe her pain. In sign language we tried to explain our concern for her tooth problem and the directions for the medication. I quickly learned that some situations are universal, especially toothaches.

Their home had a dirt floor with a stove, sink and an old dinette table. As we said our goodbyes and walked away, we decided that we would try to help them again with provisions. By the look of their home we thought them to be impoverished.

Maria found her special spot again. We stopped to pray the Rosary together. It was in a wonderful picturesque field very near to the home of the villagers we visited. We became very peaceful as we prayed. And wouldn't you know it! A flock of those chirping little birds flew past us and nestled themselves in the same bushes as they had before. Then two beautiful roosters came out from behind a barn, hobbling over to the bushes, while looking in the direction of the singing birds. At the same time we saw the cow which was penned in behind the bushes, move closer and look the same way. I was grateful to God for our afternoon together.

It was exactly what we needed. Our Lord clearly showed me that a remedy to our own distresses may be found in reaching out to others.

6

Cornelia

WHILE WAITING FOR MARIA in the dining room so we could return to church together for a scheduled talk, Maria's son Daniel came running in. He frantically shouted that Cornelia had collapsed into his mother's arms on the second floor landing, and that Maria needed my help!

Cornelia was one of three new pilgrims who had arrived in Medjugorje the previous day. They had joined our group in the dining room that evening for dinner.

I was sitting two tables away, and couldn't hear their conversation. A couple of the people at their table got upset over the attitude and conversation of one of the new ladies. Her name was Cornelia. She was apparently behaving quite strangely, using foul language, criticizing the food and generally acting up.

This type of behavior was not consistent with the environment. Our host family was quite sensitive and loving. Their only wish was to please and serve. They weren't trained hotel professionals. They treated people as if they were family, as if their

Mother was inviting her other children from all over the world to visit with her. The village community was dedicated to making Medjugorje a welcome and accessible place.

There isn't much personal profit in accommodating travelers. In fact, the work and involvement on Our Lady's behalf by the villagers is done with love and sacrifice.

Later, I learned that Cornelia was encouraged by her sister, Anna, to join her on this pilgrimage. Apparently, Cornelia had suffered from emotional difficulties for most of her life.

As the story continued to unfold over the next couple of days, I learned that Cornelia had been in and out of many hospitals. It was Anna's hope that Cornelia would receive healing in Medjugorje. It was never quite clear to us if she suffered from substance abuse or if the problem was totally emotional.

Cornelia was taken to her room. Some of the women were really frightened. Anna, Cornelia's sister, was very upset. She couldn't stay in the room with her because she was also afraid of her violent behavior. This became a real crisis for the host family and for the guests. Jozo tried to console Cornelia. He asked if she would see a doctor, but she declined. Eventually he warned her that if this behavior continued, he would have to ask her to leave. This was very difficult for Jozo. He's a very sensitive man, eager to make people happy.

"I can't believe it," Jozo exclaimed over and over again. "Nothing like this has ever happened to me." Little did he know that a few days later he would say the same thing again. The speculations in our group about Cornelia's problem ranged from mental dysfunction, to substance abuse, and/or possession. I believed that her behavior was consistent with that of addicted personalities.

Having someone potentially violent in our midst gave us grave concern. A suggestion was made that we take turns staying up all night guarding Cornelia. In my estimation all she needed was to sleep it off. The prospect of my going without sleep another night while still suffering from jet lag was not a pleasant one.

The idea of posting guards turned into an all night prayer vigil. Most of the pilgrims in our group participated. I wound up praying on two shifts, the first shift and one more around three in the morning. When we transferred over to the second shift, I went up to bed and fell asleep. A couple of hours later I was awakened prematurely by the third shift. They had lovingly decided to sing the Ave Maria between each decade of the Rosary. It was beautifully done but not conducive to sleep.

I felt close to Christ during the prayer experiences on both shifts that night. It touched me deeply to feel the love my fellow pilgrims expressed for God as they prayed. What we accomplished that evening reminded me of one of Mother Teresa's teachings: "Together we can do great things for God."

Anna stayed up and prayed all night with each shift. She was clearly a faithful and brave young woman. This was a lesson in humility for me. It also helped bond our group. Another lesson learned, was that praying together keeps people together.

Anyway, when I reached the second floor landing, Cornelia was lying on the floor in Maria's arms. When she saw me approach, she exclaimed in perfect Italian, "I can't take it anymore!" We helped her to her feet, reassuring her that everything would be alright. We escorted her back to her room. Maria and I noticed how childlike she was, a spoiled child looking for attention, acting out by throwing tantrums and speaking profanities. Yet inside she was probably frightened and lost and begging for peace!

As we neared her room she collapsed again, telling us in fluent Italian that they were starving her. I still don't know how she knew we spoke fluent Italian. She claimed she hadn't eaten. I promised to make her a sandwich and bring it to her room. While I was reassuring her and trying to get her to her feet again, Maria started to pray. When Cornelia heard a reference to Our Blessed

Mother, she immediately stood and ran to her door while angrily reciting a series of blasphemies.

My earliar diagnosis was beginning to change. It was too frightening for me to think that evil could get that close to a human being. Feeling a tremendous urge to wash my hands, I quickly made her a sandwich and brought it up to her room, knocked, but got no answer. From outside the door I told her that I was leaving her the food I had promised, then I quickly left.

Jozo told me later that she had put her cigarette out in the food. He had to ask her to leave that evening as she was becoming increasingly abusive. He called her a taxi and she left for the city of Mostar. We were all relieved.

Cornelia, possesed a flair for the dramatic. It seemed as if I was encountering many situations and people that spoke deeply to my psyche. Apparently, I was being called to confront all the demons that had haunted me throughout my life. I had had my share of controlling women in both my childhood and young adult life and Cornelia's strong will spoke to that.

I was being shown that I had more courage, ability, and support from God than I thought I had. I was able to deal with and overcome whatever came along. To my surprise, I was not only handling it, but at the same time I was doing the Lord's work and experiencing positive results.

Our Lady was taking me back to the days of my youth so I could grow and see myself as capable of accepting the challenges of life, like learning to ride a bike without training wheels. She was teaching me to accept the falls and bruises, and eventually celebrate the success of riding freely. Medjugorje was becoming an emotional and spiritual boot camp for me. Our Lady was my drill instructor.

7

Miracles Are Forever

As Gail and I left the church, she asked if I had prayed by the cemetery yet. I told her that I hadn't and maybe I would go right now. As I walked through the fields in back of the church in the direction of the cemetery, I saw three people ahead of me in the distance.

I thought to myself "Gee it would have been nice if I had the cemetery all to myself, to pray privately." Nearing; the cemetery, I followed them as they entered. We entered a tree lined path, adjacent to the cemetery wall. The entrance to it was around the corner of the wall. The people ahead of me turned the corner first. Following them around the corner, I found that they had stopped and were looking up towards the sun. They were excitedly shouting, "Look! Look! How beautiful!" I looked up towards the sun and it hurt my eyes so I immediately looked away.

Then something inside of me said, "If they can see something, then you can too!" And I did! Words could never describe what I saw when I looked up again. The sun had eclipsed! I'm a little color-blind and I had sunglasses on but I believe that the darkened center was probably reddish in color.

As I continued to look I was overwhelmed! There were streams of fire all around it. It was an awesome sight!

I was overjoyed and afraid at the same time. I learned that the human mind has great difficulty understanding the supernatural. I dropped to me knees thanking and praising Jesus. I was moved to the core of my very being. I felt so special and loved. We all shared this experience together. Later I learned they were Sheila and Richard Petrucci and Edward Melucci from Rhode Island. Apparently, these people had seen this happen before, so they were getting quite a kick out of my excitement.

Then all of a sudden a big spiral, like a tunnel, came out of the sun and with enormous speed dashed towards earth. I jumped back, as if it would reach me, but it stopped. It was again a dark color, probably red with bands of gold. As this happened the center of the sun turned into what appeared to be the Host.

Sheila asked me what I was seeing. As I described it to her, she told me I was seeing the full blown version of the miracle of the sun. She said she and her husband had seen it before on a previous trip. Continuing to look, we all saw the Host in the center and then I started to see the Crown of Thorns forming at the top. Overtaken with joy, praising God and Jesus and Mary, I did not know who to thank first. I would turn my eyes away, thinking that it would disappear, that it was an illusion, but it didn't go away.

Sheila, Richard and Ed later estimated that we all looked into the sun for about seven or eight minutes. While we were in the middle of this experience, Sheila picked up a rock that was at my feet. It had a distinct marking of a cross cut into it. She gave it to me as a remembrance of this wonderful afternoon. I told her she should keep it, but she insisted that I take it. She had found one on her last visit. I was ecstatic! Sheila also mentioned that Our Lady was said to provide these rocks with crosses throughout the

Medjugorje area.

Overjoyed, we all hugged each other and prayed together in thanksgiving. I still couldn't believe that I was worthy of the gifts I was receiving. As the sun returned to normal, we started to walk out of the cemetery back towards the church.

We saw a young couple who had come to the cemetery to look at the sunset together. They were leaning with their backs on a large tombstone, looking directly at the sun. I asked them if they had seen anything. They said they hadn't. I was shocked! They were sitting front row center! Still perplexed by their answer, I asked again, "Are you sure you didn't see anything?" The young man responded briskly and said, "I believe you. Why don't you believe me?" I quickly realized that you have to want to have God in your life, in order to search for him and find him (Mt 7:7).

The three of us continued walking. Reaching the vinyard we met the pastor of the Church of St. James. He was taking a leisurely stroll through the field with another Franciscan friar and a visiting German priest. We asked them to pose with us for pictures while we stopped to say hello. I made very sure at this point to ask for my companions' names and addresses; these good people were going to be part of me for the rest of my life. I will never forget them.

We were so happy and full of peace that we didn't even mention the experience to the priests. It's funny, I know what we witnessed was awesome by human standards. Yet, in a way it was natural. I got a sense that we are very much connected to the supernatural experience, but on a different level of consciousness. It's as if the Lord lifted the blinders from our eyes and gave us a glimpse of His life-support attached to our souls.

As we left the priests, I realized that they must experience this every day. Medjugorje is a place where miracles are as common as taxi cabs are in New York City.

This experience was not only given to me and those who visit Medjugorje, but, to every one of God's children. He reassures us of His love. He gives us these great signs to bolster our faith. He wants us to turn to Him in a deeper relationship.

These experiences are a vision of our royal inheritance as God's children. All we have to do is open the door a crack. He floods us with His graces, the graces that we need to believe, to fight temptation, and to understand His will.

I'm convinced that everyone can see these signs and each of us can change his heart and develop a relationship with God. All we need to do is reach out to Him! Nothing more is necessary than saying, "God, if you're out there, I want to know you! I want to believe in you! I want your help!"

The Rosary and Mass that evening took on greater meaning for me. I had to grow up now. There were no excuses. I could never doubt the existence of God, and that meant not succumbing to anxiety or fear or hopelessness again. God was telling me, "Al, stop trying to believe, and believe!" as Mother Angelica says. I had been so programmed with anxiety. Now that I had received this emotional and spiritual healing, my mind and body needed to get accustomed to my new heart.

Thinking disturbing thoughts that would have usually made me upset, I realized very quickly that line of thinking wasn't going anywhere. I reminded myself that God is with me, and that ultimately things will turn out (Lk 12:22).

8

Crisis and Healing

THE NEXT DAY I WENT over to inspect the passport log book hoping to retrieve mine. The log was on one of the tables in the guest house dining room. There were three passports on the table with the log and none of them were mine. I asked our hostess, Jozo's wife Merissa, where it was. "Yes, it appears to be missing!" she said, "But don't worry, we'll find it."

It was lost! Here I am in communist country in a changing political climate. They'll never let me out! I have a business to run! Panic set in, maybe even anger. (And it's not very easy to be angry in Medjugorje!)

For the next two days all the guests checked and double-checked their belongings with the hope that maybe it had gotten mixed in with their things. Jozo very patiently took me to all the shops and restaurants I had visited to see if it had been found. Nothing!

My group was scheduled to visit Father Jozo Zovko the next day but I didn't go as I was frantic over my passport. Here I was on one hand, experiencing miracles which were designed to bolster and increased my faith and belief in God. Yet on the other hand, I was allowing hopelessness to enter my heart. Oh how slowly we learn! Now I know how St. Peter felt when he denied Our Lord three times (Mt 26:31). Where was my faith?

This kindhearted man, Jozo, felt very badly for me. He drove me to the town of Citluk to report the missing passport to the police. The police station appeared familiar to me — like I had been there before. This was the same station that the visionaries were intially brought to for questioning. It was in the video I had seen. Recalling that this part of the documentary always seemed to hold my attention and interest more, it was uncanny that I would wind up there. In this communist country, all visitors are required to submit their passports to their host for recording purposes. The authorities continually check these records.

Fortunately, the police were able to issue me a temporary visa. Jozo's daughter had entered my passport information into the log book. I might still be there if she hadn't. Afterwards, Jozo took me to a local shop to have new passport photos taken. It was shocking to learn that there was an overnight wait for them. The concept of the one hour photo hadn't hit the Yugoslav marketplace.

My emotions were running high and low. Part of me was enjoying the experience and adventure. Another part felt a weight hanging over my head. Jozo took me to a coffee bar. We had espresso and met some of his acquaintances. All were very warm and friendly, just regular guys.

The Yugoslav banking system was an experience. Bank customer accounts are still kept on handwritten index cards. The people waiting on line had serious expressions on their faces. U.S. banks are all computerized. It occurred to me, that in our high-technology society we don't get to see faces and communicate personally anymore. We live in a time of recorded messages and computer decision-making. Processes that cannot distinguish feeling and allow compassion.

While in Citluk I asked Jozo if we could go to a supermarket. Supermarket would not be the word to use to describe the store Jozo took me to. It was a kind of department and grocery store combination. There were no decorations or manikins. Its appearance was drab. I wanted to buy some things for that poor family Maria and I had met.

Looking at the prices I noticed how very expensive things like coffee and chocolate were. Also, clothing was as high as it is in our own American department stores, but the standard of living in Yugoslavia makes these purchases prohibitive for the average family.

Because of Jozo's warmth and care he could help me forget my dilemma at times. I feared getting a new passport wouldn't be quite as easy as getting a temporary visa. He took me for lunch in the same restaurant our tour group had taken his lovely family to dinner a few days earlier. We enjoyed our lunch together. Jozo is an extrovert, very bright, with a deep love for God. When you meet poeple like him you know why Our Lady chose to visit Medjugorje. Jozo tried to break the news gently, that I might have to either fly or take a twelve hour train ride alone to Zagreb. This is where the closest American Consul is located.

On our way home from lunch, Jozo kept asking me who the needy villagers were that I told him about earlier. I tried to describe their house, but he couldn't figure out who they were. He practically insisted that we go to their house. I really would have preferred to go back there with Maria, but to satisfy his curiosity or overprotectiveness, I directed him to the house. When he saw it he explained that he knew the people and they weren't poor. They were living in this building temporarily. He pointed to their new three story home, with guest facilities, which was under construction nearby.

He mentioned to me that he knew of two aged widows who could sorely use help so we went to their home. When we arrived he called out to them from the entrance way. A frail, elderly peasant woman came out of the house.

He greeted her by her name, Dreana, and handed her the carton of things that Maria and I had bought, explaining in Croation that it was a gift. She was dumbfounded as she looked at the contents. She had a grateful look on her face. I didn't know what to say. She asked him to ask me what she could give to me in return. I told him a kiss.

She kissed me warmly on both cheeks and hugged me. It felt as if Jesus were hugging me. She took my hands into hers and squeezed them firmly. I knew in my heart that those calloused hands of her's were a tribute to her endurance of a hard life. A life sustained by faith and trust in God. The three of us were choked with emotion and tears.

Our Lady was continuing to lead me, guiding, teaching and directing me throughout this journey. She was showing me that God knows our state of being and has compassion for us. Jozo was a real blessing to me, as we shared many close moments together. He was like my guardian angel.

The prospects of a twelve hour train ride alone through a communist country, without a passport, was not very appealing to me. As I walked to church later that day panic set in again. Everyone was telling me that the passport would turn up. They were all praying for me. With all the miracles happening there, it had to show up. Yet somehow inside I knew that the Lord was calling me to another experience.

Approaching the church I saw Father Svet, remembering his face from seeing him on many of the videos about Medjugorje. The thought came to me, maybe if I asked him to pray for me, my passport would turn up. Introducing myself and shaking his hand, I explained what had happened. He said confidently, "Forget about it, Armando. Come in church now and listen to my talk."

Incredibily, the topic of his talk was crisis and our relationship to God in those times. After the talk I met Father outside the church again and thanked him. He is so very kind, and humble. He was kind enough to autograph a copy of a book I had purchased, called, "Pray with the Heart" writing:

> *Armando! God bless you and thank you for your pilgrimage!*
>
> *Fr. Svetozar Kraljevic, O.F.M.*

Imagine thanking me for the pilgrimage! Talk about humility! He also gave me the telephone number and name of an American seminarian at the seminary in Zagreb. He suggested I call him when I arrived there and try to arrange to get together with him for company. Father Svet also promised to include me in his prayers.

Later Maria and I met Sister Francis who was sitting on a bench opposite the church tower where the apparitions take place. We sat and talked awhile. Just before saying our Rosary together, we spotted Marija Pavlovic, one of the visionaries, walking towards the choir loft door.

Apparently she was on her way to Our Lady's apparition. Her brother was at her side. We walked up to them and I handed Marija some petitions addressed to Our Lady from friends and family at home. I only said, "Hello"' and thanked her. As she took them in her hand, she seemed to be heavy in thought, perhaps preparing for her visit with Our Lady. She had an expression of concern on her face.

As we sat back down again on the bench, I thought of the secrets that Our Lady had given the children, secrets apparently related to possible future catastrophic events. The weight on their minds at times must be quite heavy. These young people are just like we are, subject to the ups and downs and pressures of life. Yet now they have an added concern for all humanity, and the responsibility of delivering Our Lady's urgent message of conversion.

At the time of the apparitions Maria and I seemed to be able to see an outline of Our Lady under the window of the apparition room. We cried with joy. We dropped to our knees thanking Our Lady. That evening turned out to be another beautiful and powerful component of my pilgrimage. Isn't it funny that I wound up with Maria and Sister in prayer keeping my mind off of my mounting crisis? No such thing as coincidences in Medjugorje, only Christ-incidences! Although my journey had elements of strife, Jesus was providing me with comfort through His loving children.

After the apparition, Ivan, one of the visionaries, walked by, slowing down as if he wanted to stop and talk to us. He seemed happy. He realized that we were praying and so continued on. There was a comfortable feeling inside me, acknowledging that Ivan was my brother in Christ, simply another one of my family members, who was gifted in a special way.

Earlier that day he had given our group an interview, allowing us to ask questions about Our Lady's messages. He turned out to be a normal eighteen year old young man, with a good sense of humor and an affinity for stylish dress. He confidently answered the questions that were being posed. His responses were honest, direct, and down to earth. One young man in the group asked him if there were U.F.O.'s in the universe. He smiled and waved his hand as if it were a fantasy. Don't bother yourself with that kind of stuff, he said. He reiterated Our Lady's message of prayer and conversion.

9

Father Jozo

I FELT DRAWN TO VISIT Father Jozo Zovko, and arranged a taxi for early the next morning. My driver, Mirko Džeba, was waiting for me outside the guest house.

I got to Father Jozo's church in Tihaljina just in time for Mass. There was only a small group of Italian visitors in church that morning. He spoke to them fluently in their native tongue. Fortunately for me, I was able to understand much of the talk he gave after Mass, and I derived a great deal of peace from his words. Father Jozo is a very peaceful and loving man, totally God-filled. He gave each of us a picture of Our Lady. On the back, inscribed in Italian, was Our Lady's message which translates as follows:

> *Dear children, I invite you to individual conversion. This time is for you. Without you the Lord cannot accomplish what he wants. Dear children, grow every day in prayer, always towards God. I am giving you a*

> *weapon against your Goliath. Here are five stones: 1) Pray the Rosary with your heart, 2) Eucharist, 3) Read the Bible, 4) Fasting, 5) Monthly confession.*

After Mass Father Jozo laid hands on the Italian visitors. They were asked to kneel at the altar. Not wanting to the disturb the group, I waited till they were finished and knelt down as Father finished blessing the last pilgrim, but he didn't notice me. He turned around quickly, rushing to the sacristy to console what appeared to be another troubled pilgrim. Not wanting to miss Father, I walked over and knelt by the sacristy door to wait for him.

I had the bottle of olive oil, bought in Citluk, for anointing of the sick back home, I brought it specifically for the son of very close friend who was in a terrible car accident. What a sight I must have been, a lone Italian-American, with a heavy, forlorn face, weighted down by what seemed to be insurmountable passport problems. There I was, kneeling on the altar step with an economy-size bottle of olive oil in my hands.

When Father came out of the sacristy he came straight over to me. He laid his hands on my head and prayed over me. As he completed his blessing, he began walking away. I reached out my hand to him and asked him to pray for the recovery of my lost passport. I felt that his prayers had to be answered. God had spoken directly to him, and he had experienced apparitions of Our Blessed Lady.

I wasn't letting go. I wanted my passport back! I didn't want to be alone in a strange city and I didn't want to leave the beautiful peace of Our Lady's presence two days earlier than I had to.

Father Jozo, who doesn't speak English, somehow knew that I needed help. It didn't occur to me to speak to him in Italian. He took my hand gently, as if I were a little child and walked me out of the church. He led me across the patio area and into the rectory where he introduced me to Anca, his assistant and translator.

Anca asked me my name and I told her it was Armando. She kept repeating it, over and over in a loving way, "Armando! Armando!" as she looked deeply into my eyes. I explained my passport problem, asking her to ask Father Jozo to pray for me. She warmly took my hand and led me out of the rectory across the patio to explain my situation to Father Jozo in Croation. She wrote a note for his signature to the directors of the tour, Penny Abruzzese and Mary Fistler, asking them not to let me go to Zagreb alone. Father was busy with many people who were eager to speak to him.

Not wanting to burden Father further, I reassured Anca that I would be fine and asked her to ask Father to pray for me. Anca signed the note herself. Filled with the joy of these deeply spiritual people, I prepared to leave this peaceful place, asking Anca to pray for me and my ministry back in the states. She hugged me for what seemed to be hours. Her warmth touched my heart! It felt like Our Lady was holding me.

Anca told me to go and pray on Apparition Hill. As we drove away, I heard her voice reassuring me as if she were right next to me and I cried for some time in the car driving back. Somehow Mirko the taxi driver, who turned out to be a another wonderful friend, knew how deeply touched I was by Father Jozo and Anca.

Later I was to find out that Anca had been a communist social worker who was assigned to the Medjugorje investigation by the Yugoslav government. In the process of her investigative work she had a conversion experience of her own. Leaving her job and severing her party affiliation, she joined Father Jozo in ministering to the pilgrims as his interpreter. My understanding is that her conversion story gives powerful witness to the divine grace and love of God.

10

The Local Flavor

THE TAXI DRIVER MIRKO AND I PRAYED the Rosary together as we drove. He in Croation and I in English. He asked me to visit his home in Citluk and meet his children. "Of course," I told him, honored by the invitation. When we arrived at his house we walked past a large trellis covered with grapevines.

It reminded me of the old world flavor I remembered from my youth. We lived in an immigrant Italian neighborhood in Brooklyn. No self respecting Italian-American family would not have a grapevine or fig tree from the old country growing in its backyard.

Mirko introduced me to his daughter, Morina and his son, Vladimir, who came in a short time later from school. Morina is twenty-one years old and unable to secure a job because of the current job market conditions. I began to realize as we talked that it's quite difficult for a young women her age to secure employment. Still Morina does an admirable job of caring for the household, cooking and cleaning. Mirko's wife Gubica, was at work at the time.

Mirko offered me a drink. We compared how different our lives were in our countries, yet I realized also how much alike we were, with similar hopes and dreams.

After our visit, Mirko took me to the bank again to cash travelers' checks, in preparation for my journey to Zagreb. Later we met in the coffee bar across the parking lot and had a cup of espresso and met some of his friends. Mirko and Jozo seemed to be quite popular. They knew many people. I really got the flavor of life in Yugoslavia.

Mirko took me to a roadside restaurant for lunch. As we entered the dining room, he was greeted by the staff and patrons alike. Apparently he was no stranger here either. The waiter sat us at a table near a very large fireplace hearth, which had a roaring fire. He suggested to us that we have the barbecued pork shish-ka-bob. The chef used hot cinders from the burning logs in the fireplace to roast the meat.

The owner, the waiter, and chef joined us in conversation. They didn't speak English or Italian, but we still communicated quite well. Then Mirko informed me in sign language that the woman who was sitting with them was the local prostitute. It took me by surprise! A prostitute in Medjugorje? Could that be possible? I immediately felt sad for her. There were many special signs and wonders so close to her, just a glance away! If she would only dare to look!

The others were making fun of her but I knew what a special child of God she was. I wanted to tell them that, but I was afraid I would embarrass her. When we were introduced, she made it a point to let me know that she was a Muslim. Ironically, she wanted me to know her not for being a prostitute, but for being a Muslim.

I invited her to join us for coffee. She hesitated a moment at first, then sat down. In sign language I related to her that there was one God and that we were all His children, equally loved and cherished.

She seemed relieved by this. I pray that Our Lady will touch her heart. After shaking everyone's hand and saying goodbye, I felt that they were genuinely warm and giving people. Maybe Our Lord had the same sense when he visited Matthew the tax collector's house (Mt 9:10).

# 11

Gethsemane

WHEN I RETURNED to the guest house late that afternoon, I felt drawn to go and pray on Cross Mountain, Mt. Krizevac. Anca had said to pray on Apparition hill, but it was further away and time was short.

My lonely journey to Zagreb was quickly approaching. I walked up the road a short distance and started to climb up the Cross Mountain path. To express their love for Our Lady, the villagers erected large bronze "Stations of the Cross" plaques in sequence along the path to the summit. Somewhere around the second station I sat on a rock to pray. My heart was very heavy.

This was the first time I was alone all day. The reality of taking a lonely trek through Yugoslavia was sinking in. While starting to pray I heard the voices of pilgrims coming down the path. I felt I just needed more privacy, so I started to walk a little further on and sat on another rock. A beautiful yellow butterfly was flying up and down the path. I wondered if it wasn't a little early in the season for butterflies? The weather was unusually spring like for this time of year, but it was still very cold in the mornings and evenings.

Continuing to feel the need for more seclusion, I looked around and spotted what appeared to be a doorway opening cut through a stone fence. I walked through the entryway and found myself in a perfectly flat, fenced in terraced area, a secluded garden. It had a large rock half implanted in the ground near the entryway. Sitting on this rock, I started to pray again. As the first words of the Creed left my lips, my eyes started to well up with tears and I began crying uncontrollably.

It seemed that my sobbing only stopped briefly when I ended a prayer, and commenced again, at the start of another. While praying the Rosary, all the issues that troubled me in my life started to surface in my mind.

It was an affirmation for me that the Lord knew all the intimate details of my troubles and decisions. I felt a tremendous sense of His empathy. Somehow I knew I wasn't alone. It was like a purging. It occurred to me that my experience was a correlation of my life's trials to those tribulations of Our Lord in the Gospel. I felt as if I were following Him in the Way of the Cross.

Coming to the fourth Hail Mary in the fourth decade of the Rosary, I sensed, that Our Lady was holding me in her arms. She somehow communicated to me internally that she was holding me and that with her was my deceased mother. I was deeply touched. My tears flowed like a river, coming from a spot so deep inside that I hadn't known it existed. These were tears of joy, sorrow, and discernment.

I have always kidded my friends when they've gotten overly emotional, suggesting that they should try out for a part in a tragic opera. I thought to myself, "If they could see me now!" When I finished the fifth sorrowful mystery, I heard again an inner voice telling me to relax and be at peace.

Walk around the garden! Collect yourself! Enjoy the view over the valley! While walking about, I thought about my wife and how good she was and I was grateful for my children and my wonderful friends, whose generous prayers help me achieve this healing experience.

I wanted to tell them that everything was going to be all right. That God truly loves us and that we are connected to Him in a very special way, a way that is somehow disguised from us, but still very real.

Cornelia popped into my head out of nowhere. Something was telling me to speak with her, to reassure her of Our Lady's love. I wanted to suggest to her that she should let Medjugorje touch her, and that she was going to be alright.

Little did I know that she would be in the dining room when I returned. Cornelia had come back from Mostar the day before. I greeted her and suggested that she try to relax and let Our Lady touch her heart. She looked at me rather dazed. Still experiencing some fear in approaching her, I felt compelled to relay Our Lady's message.

I didn't want to leave that garden. The peace there was incredible. Repeatedly walking around the terraced area, I discovered little purple flowers. They had a sweet perfumed smell and grew very close to the ground. I collected some rocks and parts of a bush as a remembrance.

My idea was to place the collected samples in a covered glass jar on a shelf in my study. The shelf is a kind of an altar. On it there's a statue and a picture of Our Lady next to a picture of the Sacred Heart of Jesus. I didn't realize then that these little flowers were going to have a special significance for me when I returned.

Last Christmas I shopped a little early for my wife Joan's present. So she could not peek into the box, I had it gift wrapped. The young woman at the service counter told me the Christmas wrapping had not yet arrived, so I picked out the next best thing. Joan is very fond of the color purple and they had a beautiful, all-purple combination of wrapping and decoration. The decoration was a bunch of little purple violets. After we opened our presents on Christmas, I spotted the ornamental little bunch of violets in the discarded wrappings and decided to put them in a small clay piece I made in my formation class — ("You are the potter, I am the clay" (Is 64:8). It turns out those little flowers were exactly the same color and shape as the ones I picked on Cross Mountain. These flowers were sitting next to the statue of the Blessed Mother on the shelf all this time.

I didn't understand at the time, but I now realize that this was my "Garden of Gethsemane" experience. I was being asked to give up my control and my will to God, as Jesus did. He carried His cross, I must carry mine. As I walked down that mountain I knew that my passport was not going to be found, and that I would have to proceed to Zagreb. The Lord had His reasons. I needed to understand what real trust in God was.

I noticed that the butterfly kept going up the path to the summit, preparing the way and escorting the pilgrims. I wondered how many times in my life the path was prepared for me, yet I was too blind to see. Butterflies are going to get a lot more attention from me now.

—12—

Journey to the Unknown

I TRIED EVERYTHING IN MY POWER to avoid the ride to Mostar for the connecting train to Zagreb. To get there Jozo and I had to drive across a mountain range by car. There were hairpin curves and winding roads overlooking valleys populated with houses, farms, and vineyards. Yugoslavia is stunningly beautiful, all the little cities and villages seemed to snuggle in valleys.

The thought of going to Mostar and boarding the train brought feelings of trepidation. Alone, facing the unknown, Rosary beads in hand, I called up my courage. I would be at the station in about an hour.

I felt badly for Jozo, having to drive me that distance and then return home in darkness by himself. The roads are dark and lonely after sunset. He was tired, but he tried to encourage me. He kept saying he was hoping to meet a friend at the station—maybe there would be company for me. "From your lips to God's ears, Jozo!" I thought to myself.

I had shown Anca's note to Mary Fistler while making last-minute travel arrangements with her. Mary had offered to go with me, but that would have only made me worry about her travelling back alone to Medjugorje.

We approached the city as the sky was darkening. Fortunately, there was enough light for a good look at Mostar. It's a very attractive city. The architecture has a Muslim influence. Jozo told me that the city had a fifty-percent Muslim and a fifty percent Croation Catholic population.

The streets at night are poorly lit. The station was gloomy. It was clean, but desolate. We went to the main ticket counter and Jozo helped me purchase the right ticket. Afterward we walked up two long flights of stairs to the restaurant on the upper level. The tables were on a balcony overlooking the dark and dismal central lobby of the station. I asked Jozo to have the waiter prepare sandwiches for my overnight journey. True to my Italian heritage, I had to carry food with me to feel secure and complete.

Jozo was tired but genuinely concerned for me. I was glad for his sake that the train would be leaving soon. He was under a lot of pressure the last few days, searching for the passport and helping me make the arrangements, having to deal with Cornelia, all the responsibilities of caring for thirty pilgrims in his home, in addition to tending to his normal duties in the vineyard and driving a taxi.

After the waiter brought my lunch package, I paid the check and started for the gate. Jozo then saw someone he knew, a young man standing at the gate as if he were waiting for us. Actually, he was waiting for his brother. The young men were Miki and Mario Petrovic. They were traveling on the same train on a business trip. To top it off, they spoke fluent English and Italian and immediately took me into their charge.

As we boarded the train, I hugged Jozo and thanked him. I was going to miss him. My two traveling companions showed me how to play a Yugoslav card game and, becoming good at it, I won quite a few games much to their chagrin. As we sat playing cards in their compartment, another fellow came to the cabin door. After an exchange of words in Croation, Miki informed me that he would be bunking with them. Their compartment had triple-decker beds. My sleeper was only a few doors down from them. A private compartment had been arranged for me. It would be safer since I'd be traveling alone and would be able to lock myself in when I slept. As it turned out this fellow also spoke English quite well. He was sitting outside in the conductor's seat because the cabin was small. After a while I decided to let the boys play cards together.

They didn't know how to play the game with three people. I kept winning so they weren't able to play with each other, so I stepped out to stretch my legs. Our new traveling companion, Vili Einspieler, called over to me. He pointed to the bench next to the conductor's chair where he was sitting. He was about six feet tall, slim build, had long light brown hair with deep blue eyes. I told him of my experiences in Medjugorje, referring to all the close moments I had with Our Lady and Our Lord while there and how they had affected me.

We wound up in a theological/philosophical conversation. It was fantastic! What were the odds of my meeting any of these people, let alone someone who not only had the command of the English language, but one interested in a realm of consciousness that transcended the human condition. He was inquisitive about the experience of faith. We talked about things such as: "Religion being the opiate of the poeple." It turned out that he was a Yugoslav journalist, highly educated and literate. I genuinely liked him and wanted to be his friend. He gave me his address and I promised to write and to contact him if I ever planned to return.

The message I left with him was not to try to figure things out, just let himself feel God. I told him there was no economy or politics or scholarly thought that could match the awesome sense of love and peace I had felt in Medjugorje. I am convinced that Our Lady was touching his heart through our chance meeting. He was very curious about my pilgrimage and belief. I thanked him for his company and friendship and gave him a set of blessed rosary beads from Medjugorje. He told me he would give them to his son.

It was getting late so we said goodnight and I retired to my compartment, making sure to latch my door behind me. The accommodations weren't perfectly clean, but they were passable. I layed down on my bunk and started to pray the Rosary, looking at the lights flickering by as we traveled, apprehensive, yet at the same time peaceful.

Falling asleep, I thanked the Lord for all the company He had given me thus far. He wouldn't abandon me! The next thing I knew, the conductor was knocking at my door announcing our arrival in Zagreb. Disembarking, I passed my companions' compartment and all was quiet. I didn't want to wake them to say goodbye. Hopefully they understood.

I'm going to visit their new pizza restaurant (Pizzeria Miki) when I return to Medjugorje. I promised to send them some "state side" pizza recipes. It struck me as funny that gourmet cooking happens to be one of my favorite hobbies; my specialty is homemade pizza. It's considered my trademark.

13

Zagreb

I LOOKED AT MY WATCH. It was 4:30 in the morning. Zagreb station wasn't lit up anymore than the station in Mostar. Zagreb was a bigger city. The poor lighting combined with its big buildings lent it a desolate appearance. My first thought was to call a taxi quickly and get to the hotel.

I no sooner placed my foot on the platform, then what appeared to be the only baggage attendant at Zagreb station approached me. He introduced himself as Josif Turac and understood both English and Italian. I told him I was looking for a taxi stand. He insisted that he accompany me to my hotel, and took my travel bag from my hand. I told him I was going to the Hotel Dubrovnik.

Josif claimed that the hotel was only a short walk. So there I was, walking in the wee hours in the morning, in a strange city, with my new friend Josif. He very generously shared the details of his family and Yugoslav lifestyle. The short walk turned out to be about eight blocks, through a dark and dreary commercial section of the city.

As we approached the hotel, I asked him if there was a coffee bar open. He very happily escorted me to a small place, one that was already bustling at that early hour.

We had a few cups of coffee and Josif also had a couple of whiskeys to help get the coffee down. We continued to talk about his life and my experience of Medjugorje. He explained to the waitress that I was a traveler and a pilgrim to Medjugorje.

The other people looked over at us, strange pair that we made. Here we were, the resident baggage attendant with his pushcart eight blocks away from the station, and a stranger wearing a New York Yankee baseball cap, having a few together at five in the morning.

Josif was a charming fellow. He insisted on giving me his address and a dated picture of himself. The photo must have been taken when he was about twenty years old. He inscribed on the back of it in Italian: "Armando, Per Te, (for you) Josif." He told me he was about forty. After coffee, we walked a block or two more to the Hotel Dubrovnik. Josif took me right to the front desk.

I gave him a couple of blessed religious medals and he claimed that he would try to get back and visit me later on in the evening. I paid him, thanked him, and said goodbye.

Our Lady's tour company certainly was efficient. Every step of the way I had personal tour guides, who were not only friendly but who also added to my growth experience. The hotel seemed to be a basically modern and clean facility. However, I was advised by the desk clerk that it was too early to check in and I would have to wait until evening for my room.

I asked the desk clerk if he would hold my belongings and direct me to the nearest church. He spoke English fairly well. Showing me a place to leave my bag, he then directed me to the church. I walked about two blocks, almost past the church, and saw a nun come out of what looked like an office building to open a wrought iron gate.

She spoke no English, but was able to understand that I was looking for Mass. I was early, but she invited me in. It was a very small chapel, probably designed to provide liturgy for the city office workers. It was built in marble, dimly lit, very plain. Sitting down and resting I prayed my Rosary, thanking the Lord and Blessed Mother for getting me to Zagreb safely and providing me all that I needed. About a half hour later a priest came in. I was glad for the chance to attend Mass and receive communion.

I left the church, and with some sketchy directions proceeded to the American Consulate. I stopped a couple of pedestrians, but they didn't speak English. Finally, a well-dressed woman who spoke English fluently directed me to the U.S. Embassy.

When I arrived there the Marine guard told me that the consulate was closed on Saturday. My heart started to jump. I explained about my appointment with the Vice Consul, Peter Mulrean. He asked me to wait while he telephoned Peter.

While waiting, a policeman came over to me. Apparently he was stationed on that corner to protect the consulate. He too reminded me that it was Saturday and that the consulate was closed. He questioned me about the nature of my business and I told him that I was an American and had an appointment with the Vice Consul.

Finally the Marine guard's voice came over the intercom, asking me to come back in an hour, stating that Mr. Mulrean would meet with me then. I asked him if there was a restaurant I could go to for breakfast. He directed me around the corner to a very nice coffee bar that also served food.

I ordered a sandwich and espresso and sat quietly and relaxed while looking out the big front window at a beautiful tree lined park. Zagreb was a beautiful city in daylight, clean and pleasant to the eye. The park reminded me of Gramercy Park in New York City. I stayed in the restaurant until it was time to meet with Peter.

The policeman wasn't around as I left the restaurant. I made my way quickly to the front door of the consulate, rang the bell and the Marine guard admitted me through the electronically locked door. As I came to the reception window in the outer foyer, I felt relieved. The guard asked me to leave my camera on the table.

The guard electronically searched me before admitting me to the inner reception room. He asked me to sit, and explained that Mr. Mulrean had arrived and would see me shortly. While waiting for Peter, I was worried whether or not I had sufficient identification with me to complete the new passport application.

After a while Peter came into the room and introduced himself to me. He was a collegiate-type young man, pleasant but initially business-like. After a short interview he asked me to sign a new application form. I was relieved when he also asked for the forty-two dollar fee. At that moment, I realized that my application was satisfactory and that he would issue the passport.

As I started to calm down, he informed me that I needed to go to the Yugoslav government office for the visa. He reassured me that there would be no problem, that they were expecting me and he would take me there. As we walked together, he told me that there have been many occurrences of lost or stolen American (and oddly enough Yugoslav) passports specifically in the Medjugorje area. He attributed that to the fact that the visitors there were very relaxed and caught up in the experience, their defenses were down, making it easier for a thief to operate.

We walked through the beautiful park that I had seen earlier. It was a great day and the walk was somewhat relaxing, but I was so preoccupied with the task at hand that I couldn't fully enjoy it. When we arrived at what turned out to be police headquarters we were told to wait. The person we needed to see would be there shortly. Peter kept looking at his watch. We waited about fifteen minutes while making small talk. Peter informed me that he had to leave because of another appointment. He explained that I would be fine and that what remained to be done was just routine. However, he further explained, that if a problem arose the consulate office would know where he was. He shook my hand, I thanked him and he left. There I was, alone in the lobby of the Yugoslavian police headquarters, waiting for a communist official to issue me a visa, not knowing if he or she could speak English.

My mind began to wander as I looked around at the mirror covered windows and doors. We hear so many stories about the way Americans are treated abroad. The Iranian hostages crossed my mind, among other things.

A well dressed woman entered the station. She addressed me in English, asking me for my newly-issued passport and the temporary visa issued in Citluk. She reviewed the papers and said that she would return shortly. I followed her out the front door and watched her command the police guard to open a door to one of the buildings down the street. He took out his key, opened the door for this lady and another lady who was waiting outside the station house. He locked the door and positioned himself by it.

Now I was thinking that I had neither passport, nor visa in my possession. It occurred to me how we take things for granted when we travel. We're at the mercy of the country we're visiting, and if they should arbitrarily cause us trouble we are isolated from help.

After waiting another fifteen minutes or so, I saw the police guard open the door with his key and let the women out. The woman who had spoken to me walked over and handed me my passport with the visa certification. I thanked her and asked her if she had been to Medjugorje. She responded by looking me straight in the eye and stating emphatically that she was an athiest, and gave me a look that said to me: "Don't push it, buddy."

I felt relieved as a I walked back toward my hotel, thinking how sad God must feel at being rejected by His children. This lady seemed to have a lot going for her, with many gifts God had given her. She had talent and position along with physical beauty, and yet she was blind to His existence and true beauty.

As I continued to make my way back, it amazed me how comfortable the people were in the coffee bars. It seemed to be their way of life. Men and women would come in alone or with friends, order a drink or a coffee, sit, read, talk. Nobody pressured them to buy anything or to vacate their seat. It's a socially accepted enterprise. People seemed to find time to sit and chat together.

They didn't appear to be as rushed or preoccupied as Americans are. However, I didn't find them to be overly friendly with strangers. I walked down the street, hearing people uttering the word for stranger in their language as they spotted me in my New York Yankee baseball cap. The Yugoslav word is very similar in pronunciation to the Italian word for stranger, "Stranieri."Not one person smiled.

There must have been some tension in the people because of the political climate. While resting in the hotel that afternoon, I heard noises coming from what I thought were guests in the room above me. It seemed like they were yelling out their window, laughing and throwing out small pieces of paper.

Later, I decided to go for another walk. Earlier I had seen a Cathedral through my window that I wanted to try and visit. I got to the lobby and approached the desk clerk and told him about the disturbance. He said to forget it! It was propaganda! I told him it came from the floor above me.

He smugly informed me that my room was on the top floor. I think he thought that it came from a helicopter. It's my guess that it was coming from the roof. While having dinner that evening, I also heard some shouting from the street below us, by a large group of young people.

Not only was I waylayed in a foreign land, I found myself in a strange city with limited ability to communicate, with dwindling funds, and right smack in the middle of political protests, complete with propaganda!

This was further confirmed when I visited the coffee bar again later. Two well-dressed gentlemen engaged me in conversation, half in English and half in Italian. We talked about Medjugorje. I witnessed to them, but they had very little knowledge of what was happening there. I gave them each a religious medal which was blessed in Medjugorje. They immediately wore them. As I continued to share with my new friends, I noticed that they had been drinking a great deal, but they were very cordial and friendly. One of the fellows asked me my opinion of the Yugoslav people. Did I know that their political climate was in a state of flux?

My answer to him was based on my experience in Medjugorje with meeting some of the locals. I responded by saying that the Yugoslav people had a lot of heart. I found them to be a talented and gifted people. A people that would successfully weather these changes with their usual hard work and patience.

I continued, saying that they were an ancient culture with a great deal of experience. The fellow seemed to be relieved by my observations. In my travels I have gotten the feeling that Americans are a hard act to follow. We are considered successful and wealthy and we tend to overshadow countries by our reputation.

It must be hard for people to understand our type of freedom. We have a freedom that allows everyone the chance to succeed and prosper, the best of us and the worst of us. Success may not be easy, but it's attainable. I probably could have remained in the discussion all afternoon, but I wanted to stroll a little and get more of the flavor of the city.

Continuing my walk I ran into what appeared to be a fast-food hamburger joint. The name was "Ham! Ham!" It was styled like our McDonald's. People seemed to enjoy it there as much as they do here. I noticed however that the shopkeepers or vendors sometimes became impatient with me when I handed them my money and asked them to take what I owed to them. Yugoslavian money was very difficult to figure out. Bills that say 5000 are literally worth five cents.

Zagreb is a cozy, little city with almost all main thoroughfares leading to a central plaza. The plaza has cable cars, fine stores and restaurants. The architecture is both old ornate and modern style.

Finally, I found the cathedral, named after St. Peter. It was magnificent. There were stone sculptures of people and animals in the front of the church. Their facial expressions were still very life-like even after eight hundred years sitting in the elements.

As I attempted to enter, a gypsy woman jumped in front of me, from nowhere, to beg for money. I was so startled that I waved her away. She was no more than four foot ten, but she made me uncomfortable. I was not feeling all that secure to begin with, certainly not so sure of my safety, to expose money in public. My old South Brooklyn survival defenses were engaged.

The cathedral was beautiful inside. The paneling and woodwork amazed me. The altar appeared to be constructed of gold. There were beautiful icons. I took a few pictures and realized that I was out of film, so I left the cathedral to try to buy more, but the stores near the cathedral were closed. After walking further and further away from the church in my search, it dawned on me that most stores probably closed in the early afternoon on Saturday.

Frustrated about being out of film, I decided to return to my hotel to see if there were any messages. Upon checking in I had called the young American seminarian in Zagreb whom Father Svet had recommended. I could either visit with him or invite him to dinner to pass the time. I was looking forward to meeting with him and the other young seminarians.

Mary Fistler told me that one seminarian had been a wealthy and successful Wall street stock broker, who had visited Medjugorje while on a business trip. After returning to his home in the states, he was unable to readjust to his previous lifestyle.

Apparently, he gave his money and possessions away and flew back to Medjugorje penniless, throwing himself on the mercy of the Franciscans. Unfortunately for me, they were unable to meet me that day because they were having difficulty securing a confessor in Zagreb who spoke English.

Sitting in my hotel room that afternoon, I started to get lonely, so I decided to pray the fifteen decades of the Rosary as I had done each night in the church of St James in Medjugorje. I placed a small free standing crucifix on the night stand, knelt down and looked at my watch. It was exactly the same time they start the Rosary at the church in Medjugorje.

At the hour that Our Lady usually appears, I noticed that the same smell I was accustomed to in Medjugorje, the smell of burning vine branches was coming in through the window. I immediately felt blessed and safe.

After finishing the Rosary, I read for a while, then dressed for dinner and took the elevator down to the restaurant. Surprisingly there were very few people at the restaurant for a Saturday night. The price of dinner was consistent with the average restaurant at home. The waiter seated me at the table of my choice. Fortunately he spoke fluent English and Italian.

He was an interesting young fellow. We talked about Medjugorje and an assortment of subjects. He told me that he was at one time a professional soccer player. He was great company. The restaurant wasn't busy so we had a good opportunity to talk.

He mentioned that his family had a summer home in Dubrovnik, which is close to Medjugorje. He said that he would try and visit Medjugorje as soon as his work schedule permitted.

After dinner, I went down to the main lobby to ask the desk clerk to arrange for a wake up call and a taxi to the airport in the morning. My adventure was almost finished. In a few short hours, I would be on my way home.

14

Traveling Home

THE SUN WAS BEGINNING TO RISE when I arrived at the airport. It was quiet. The shops were closed as well as the ticket counters. Airport employees were coming in slowly. It worried me that the tour operator might not have arranged my return flight. So I waited apprehensively until I finally spotted a Pan Am employee, who informed me that everything was fine. While checking in, however, I was told that my reserved seat had been given to another passenger because of my changed schedule.

I knew as I boarded the 727 that I couldn't sit with Anne and Diane who had already boarded in Dubrovnik. When I saw them I was gloating. "Are you okay?" they asked. "I'm terrific," I replied. There were people behind me waiting to move on to their seats, so we agreed to talk in Frankfurt.

When I reached my seat there was someone in it. He turned out to be American. I sat next to him and he introduced himself as Michael Murphey, a wholesale jeweler from Pennsylvania. He was traveling around the world with two other fellows, and explained that they were starting to get on one another's nerves. I gave him an account of my pilgrimage to Medjugorje. He mentioned that he and his friends had stopped there for about five or six hours. They were not touched by the experience of being there. He explained that he was an agnostic, but that He wanted to experience God in his life and was interested in my account. As I continued to share with him, I realized that he knew very little about Medjugorje; they had passed through too quickly on one of those prearranged tour stops. He hadn't spent time alone, letting go, praying or trying to relate to God.

I gave him reading material, suggesting to him that he may want to return there. I cautioned him, as my friend Bob had cautioned me, to let Medjugorje happen for him. I told him that conversions were a common occurrence and shared Mary Fistler's and the young seminarian's conversion stories, and the many healings — physical, emotional, and spiritual — that pilgrims had experienced.

I shared how Medjugorje had changed my life. I explained that I was different now and that my life had a purpose. Fitting into God's plan I and had come to know how much He loves us, and realize that God desires our love and a relationship with us. This is no different than any other normal father who wants his children to love him and be part of his life experience.

As I continued to relate Our Lady's message to him I could see a keen interest developing. I explained that prayer is the link. It's our communication with Our Father in heaven. Our Lady's message is a simple one: prayer (talk to me); conversion (change your heart, include me in your life); fasting (block out the things that distract you from knowing me); and Mass and communion (know that I am with you). I was convinced when we said goodbye in Frankfurt, that he would journey again someday to Medjugorje, just as I will.

It was overwhelming to see how Our Lady had continued to care for me. She kept me company and gave me work to do at every juncture. By connecting the encounters and the fruits they bore, I would have to say that Our Lady sparked my growth. I'm convinced that the seed of her love was planted in each and every one of her children I met. The flight home was long and tiring, however it was time I needed to sort out the events of my journey.

There were emigrants on the plane from Eastern Block countries. They were traveling to a free land for asylum, much as my parents and others of their generation had done many years before. I could tell that for most of them this was their first airplane ride.

They were afraid, nervously walking around the plane in wonder and placing their faith in God. I'm sure that they hadn't had the benefit of subliminal relaxation tapes or how-to-fly books.

Photo by Adam Leskowicz. Reproduced with permission.
1. First view of Medjugorje as bus crosses small bridge that marks the entrance into the village.

2. Pilgrims gathered in prayer at the foot of the cross atop Mt. Krizevac.

Photo by Adam Leskowicz. Reproduced with permission.

3. Typical village farmhouse adds to the charm of the village.

4. Country road that leads to Apparition Hill in the village of Bijakovici.

5. Anne Cook (left), with author Al Minutoli and Diane Trupia. Photo taken in the apparition room next to the sanctuary in St. James' Church, Medjugorje.

6. Gail Yorkowitz with the author at the entry way of the church tower where the apparitions take place today.

7. Pilgrims Ed Melucci, Sheila and Richard Petruzzi in the vineyard near the cemetery.

8. Deacon Bob Campbell sitting with the author on a bench opposite the church tower, catching up on old times.

9. Visionary Vicka stopping to speak with pilgrims and accepting their prayer petitons for the Blessed Mother.

10. Maria Cenatiempo on the way to the home of the peasant woman in need of medication for a tooth ailment.

11. Jozo (top), next to his mother, sister-in-law Nevenka (left), his wife Merissa and their children.

12. Jelena with tour guide Gordana, answering questions for our pilgrim group on the porch steps of her home.

13. Outdoor Mass in the gazebo at the rear of the church.

14. Jozo with his friends and family enjoying a traditional holiday dinner of roasted kid as they celebrated the Feast of the Triumph of the Cross.

Photo by Adam Leskowicz. Reproduced with permission.
15. Goats grazing on the steep rocky path at the foot of Apparition Hill.

Photo by Adam Leskowicz. Reproduced with permission.
16. Area of apparitions near the top of Podbrdo (Apparition Hill).

Photo by Adam Leskowicz. Reproduced with permission.
17. Church of St. James, Medjugorje.

18. Father Jozo speaking to pilgrims in St. James' Church. The wood sculpture of the crucified Christ was carved out of a tree by a parishioner.

19. The serene village of Medjugorje nestled in the valley with Mt. Krizevac (Cross Mountain) as its backdrop.

20. Anca, Father Jozo's assistant and interpreter, as she handed me a note for Mary and Penny.

21. Father Jozo's picture given to me by Penny and Anca.

22. Father Svetozar Kraljevic with the author after Father's inspiring and reassuring talk.

23. Visionary Ivan after his interview with our pilgrim group.

24. Vicka at her home speaking to our pilgrim group.

25. Ivan at his home.

26. Vicka at her home.

27. Our pilgrim group, praying at he foot of the cross, atop Apparition Hill.

28. Penny Abruzzese (front left) Director of our sponsoring group, "Our Lady Queen of Peace Prayer Group", Long Island, New York. Pilgrims: Molly and Joe Burd (left) Dottie and Bernie Kennedy with Spiritual Director, Dominican Father James Moyna.

29. Matthew gathering figs on the family property, for Marie and me.

30. Tour guides Mary Fistler and Gordana.

31. The author with his traveling companions Marie, Carol, and Vince, standing at the rear of the church prior to the evening Croation Mass.

32. Photo taken by the author of his friends, Marie, Carol, and Vince standing by the cemetary as they viewed the miracle of the sun.

PART TWO

In dangers, in doubt, in difficulties, think of Mary, call upon Mary. Let not her name depart from your lips, never suffer it to leave your heart. And that you may more surely obtain the assistance of her prayer, neglect not to walk in her footsteps. With her for guide, you shall never go astray; while invoking her, you shall never lose heart; so long as she is in your mind, you are safe from deception; while she holds your hand, you cannot fall; under her protection you have nothing to fear; if she walks before you, you shall not grow weary; if she shows you favor, you shall reach the goal.

St. Bernard of Clairvaux

15

Return to Medjugorje

THERE I WAS, JOURNEYING BACK to what author Wayne Weibel refers to as the "edge of heaven." I found myself snugly seated aboard another Pan Am 747 taxiing down the runway, anticipating the powerful thrust of those massive jet engines as they vault me into the heavens. I was traveling back to Yugoslavia and that wonderful place of peace and special grace, Medjugorje. This time, I was leading a group of pilgrims, including two priests and two Pan Am flight attendants, who were seeking their God and His love and consolation, just as I did a few months earlier.

Preparing for my return trip, I experienced doubt and fear once more. Could I handle being on that aircraft? Would I be able to pull it off again? Was I going to crack this time? How dare I lead a group of pilgrims, people who were counting on me, who needed my support.

I was disturbed by my lack of faith and confidence, especially after what I had received and experienced at Medjugorje, the wonderful miracles, healings and graces. Troubled by these thoughts, I felt drawn to reconciliation, needing to confess my lack of trust in God. I asked myself how I could possibly worry this way, when God had clearly shown me how much He loved me and was part of my life (Jn 14:1).

Expecting to be admonished by the priest in the confessional, I was surprised with the genuine love and concern he showed me. He reminded me of our vulnerability as human beings, subject to the temptations and the confusion which Satan employs. Using any means Satan tries to disrupt our lives and keep us away from a relationship with God. He pointed to Scripture passages, where we are told of the many tribulations and temptations that Our Lord Jesus suffered. He referred to the hardships of the Apostles who followed Him. Perseverance in prayer was our only defense.

Father was echoing Our Lady's message. He shared his own life, disclosing times of his own weakness and inner conflicts, and how he had resorted to prayer. He explained that we shouldn't expect immediate results from prayer. In prayer, we make God a conscious part of our life, the good and the bad, as we do when we confide in friends. We need to trust in Him and then ultimately everything will turn out right. I felt uplifted as I left. Grateful to him and God, I was encouraged and energized to answer Our Lady's call again.

As the date of my departure neared, anxiety periodically cropped up. It seemed that everything was going wrong — leaks in the house, finances tightening, problems with the children, etc. At those times I asked for the prayers of my friends in my spiritual community. One woman from our parish prayed over me on two separate occasions. Both times I felt peaceful, as if a burden were lifted from me. When I finally sat in the limo bound for the airport, I was free of all anxiety and trepidation. My prayers had been answered.

As Father Louis prepared to say Mass in the airport lounge and the group gathered, a young woman approached me, volunteering to play her flute (recorder) for us during the service. As I introduced her to Father, he became a bit distracted by the unusual offer, but graciously accepted her service.

She participated in the Mass with great zeal, anxious to offer her gift. The Mass was beautiful, a perfect send-off. Afterwards, we took a picture of the group surrounding Father and his makeshift altar. The young girl approached me again asking me to send her a copy of the picture. I gave her my note pad and she wrote down her address. Her name was Heike and she was from East Germany. She also told me that she wasn't Catholic but that she was moved by our exuberance and willingness to serve. We hadn't even boarded the plane and we had already experienced a close moment with Our Lady. Her gentle hand was gathering her children and their individual gifts together.

A couple of my traveling companions had read a copy of the first draft of this book. Recalling the worry I had expressed about flying on my first trip, they periodically visited me as we were flying. They were surprised to see how calm I was throughout the flight. As flight attendants themselves, they knew first-hand how terrifying flying can be to some people. But not to me anymore!

We arrived at Dubrovnik airport on schedule without incident. A bus was waiting for us. It was exciting to see Gordana, the young tour guide from my last trip. She was waiting with a smile and greeted me with a kiss as we exited customs. Thinking that in a couple of hours we would be there, I couldn't wait to attend Mass and thank Our Lady and to see Jozo and his family again.

I asked myself if I was expecting too much from my second trip. Would Medjugorje have the same impact on me, or would it be anticlimatic? Those thoughts were dispelled when I saw the expression of love on Jozo's wife, Merissa's face, as I entered the guest house. She hugged me warmly as she called out my name, Armando. I had received the first sign of Our Lady's peace and welcome at Medjugorje. I was home again.

Mary Fistler, Gordana, Penny and I helped get the pilgrims situated in their rooms. I was impatient and wanted so much to go to church. After finally getting everyone settled, we quickly left our luggage in our respective rooms and went to the church. It was exhilarating to walk down that quaint winding country road into the valley towards the church of St. James. We could see it in the distance.

The church was completely filled, but I was able to kneel behind the last pew. The singing in Croation rang throughout my body. I had made it again! This time I felt peace and resolve, conscious at that moment of the real healing that had taken place within me.

As I prayed my first Rosary, I noticed a young man about seventeen or eighteen entering the church. He had lost all his hair. He was probably a cancer patient who was being treated with chemotherapy and I decided to offer up my Rosary for him, asking God for healing.

16

Reminiscences and Miracles

THIS GROUP WAS MORE CONGENIAL than the one on my first trip. Both priests, Father Lou and Father Jim, had a great sense of humor. Father Lou was the extrovert, the life of the party. In contrast was Father Jim, the dry-humored, with a poker face, yet sensitive and warm like a big teddy bear. He and I had great fun verbally fencing with each other.

We met the other pilgrims who were staying at our place. They were also friendly and willing to share our company. I was especially blessed by the companionship of Carol and Vince Mazurek and Marie Sterbenz. They were from my parish but we hadn't known one another well; however, we hit it off instantaneously and developed a bond. It was as if Our Lady had matched us perfectly. We were able to offer one another the support and encouragement we needed at times. They were a big part of the peace and joy I experienced.

After the English Mass the next morning, we were given orientation by Mary Fistler. As she talked, I remembered how much her story had touched me when I had my first orientation. She was still glowing. It was so very nice to be in her company again. She is really devoted to Our Lord. Afterwards, Mary, who had the responsibility of guiding us that day, marched us through the vineyards in the valley which were ladened with ripened grapes. On our way we passed wild fig trees, also heavy with fruit.

We were heading in the direction of Bijakovici, a village in the parish of Medjugorje, to visit the visionary Ivan Dragicevic at his home. As we congregated outside his patio, I felt the anticipation of the group, remembering how I had felt seeing the visionaries for the first time.

Ivan came out of the house neatly dressed and appearing serene. He led us in prayer and answered our questions with patience and thoroughness. It was thrilling to be in his company again. He made me realize how much I had grown since seeing him last. I looked at him as a brother with a common spiritual bond. What was important now, was for me to continue to live out Our Lady's messages.

After our visit with Ivan, Mary Fistler led us to the spot where Our Lady had first appeared. Standing on the road at the foot of Apparition Hill, she pointed out how steep the climb was. We marveled at how the visionaries as young children, could run up that hill, towards the beckoning Madonna, with the ease of gazelles, as the story went.

Mary advised us that it was lunch time so we would not climb the hill as a group. If any of us were willing to skip lunch we could climb on our own. Carol, Marie, Vince and I elected to climb. We walked up the road to the path, reciting the Rosary as we began our ascent.

I remembered the emotional heaviness I had the first time I climbed. The doubt I had carried with me then was now a faint memory. I was confident during the climb and resigned to the fact that I didn't need to witness miracles; they had already happened for me. Nothing could shake my belief in God now. My wish was to have a deeper, more spiritual relationship with Him, to know Him, and to understand His will for me.

When we reached the top I felt comfortable and at home. We were filled with joy and peace as we walked on this holy ground. Making our way towards the cross that marks the spot of the apparitions, my companions were concerned about my vertigo. I reassured them that I was fine, confidently standing atop the hill looking over the valley's checkerboard fields, taking in its beauty, without the slightest discomfort.

Standing there, looking at the church and village in the distance, I could sense that Our Lady was embracing the entire valley, as if the mountains surrounding the valley were her extended arms. I bent down to kiss the rocks at the foot of the cross, thanking God for giving me the grace to be standing there again.

We headed in different directions, looking for a solitary place to pray. As Carol and I later drifted back, we found ourselves a few paces from the cross where pilgrims had gathered, and quietly noticed the deep faith they had as they fervently prayed.

Then Carol looked up at the sun which was directly above our heads, and with great excitement in her voice she said, "Look at that," telling me that she saw it spinning. I tried to look but had difficulty keeping my balance. Glancing away, I saw a sunspot turn into the shape of a beautiful puffy white lamb. Encouraged, I ventured to look into the sun once more and saw it spinning. We both started to spontaneously praise and thank Jesus and Mary. How thrilling! How blessed we were to see this manifestation of God's love again.

Upon hearing our shouts of joy, Vince made his way back toward us, but he was unable to see it. He tried but it wasn't happening for him. I told him to relax, that it would come. Still, he was disappointed.

Looking away from the sun, I saw golden spots turn into crosses. The gold color was like no other I have ever seen; it was very rich and deep. As I gazed at people on the hill, the golden crosses rested on them, covering their entire torsos. All of a sudden, I started to see splashes of golden light on people's heads and shoulders. I automatically pointed at them saying: "Look gold! There's gold all over you," at the same time praising God and thanking Jesus. I must have been a spectacle.

Behind me was a Filipino woman standing next to her husband. Her forehead was covered with gold. While pointing to her, I shouted "Gold! Gold!" Her teenage son was standing nearby and he was wearing a hat. This was the same boy I had seen in church the night before, the boy who had lost his hair. As if pulled by a magnet, I moved to him, put my arm around his shoulder and began to pray. I don't know how the words came out. Then he put his head on my shoulder and began crying with abandon, the same way I had cried while praying the Rosary in that garden terrace on Cross Mountain. His parents joined us, along with another Filipino woman, and we continued to pray over him. I don't know how long it lasted or what we prayed, but I know we were all touched by God's love.

When we finished, the lady led me by the hand to another woman, who was sitting at the foot of the Cross. She asked me to pray over her too. I greeted her with a hug and kiss and began praying over her. Again, I don't know for how long. When I stopped praying she asked me to pray over another woman, but I became uncomfortable, and said that I hadn't done this before and had no special gift.

She said she realized that it was new to me, but claimed that she felt the magnetism drawing me to the young boy further intimating that the Lord might have been using me. She encouraged me again to pray over this other woman, and I did (Jn 17:9).

Afterward we embraced and kissed each other warmly, knowing that we had experienced a close moment together with

Christ. This was a moment of true prayer. I rejoined my friends. We hugged each other too and made our way down the hill saying the Rosary in thanksgiving.

Later that afternoon when we returned to the guest house, my buddies reminded me that when we came up the hill we had passed a large group of people praying over someone. There was a crowd of people around the person. I hadn't noticed for whom the prayers were intended. I stopped and extending my hands toward the center of the group and began to pray with them. Carol joined me. As we prayed, I felt a tingling in my hands like electrical energy. They said it was the same boy I was drawn to pray over. Ironically, I didn't even get his name.

After resting awhile, we decided to walk through the fields to church. Making our way between houses and chicken coops we finally found a path which led us through vineyards and farm land. As we walked, I noticed how our conversation took on deeper meaning as we confided in one another and bared our souls.

Marie and I began talking about our childhoods, families and relationships. Our Lady's healing process had begun. We began ministering to one another as we walked behind our fearless leader, Vince (who led with the spirit of an adventurer).

It was beautiful to see how openhearted they were. I was happy that Our Lord had utilized me in His call to them. They were responding to Him with childlike love and anticipation (Mt 11:25).

Eventually we came to a stand of trees and I realized that we were at the cemetery. As we turned in the direction of the church, Carol looked up and said, "The sun's spinning again." We all looked up and saw it too. It was not only spinning but changing colors. Carol and Marie also noticed little red sweethearts circling it. They were beaming with joy. The center of the sun darkened as if it had been eclipsed. Vince was more cautious as he wasn't wearing sunglasses. He looked up at the phenomena then quickly looked away, happy but fearful. I empathized with him. It really boggles the mind when you are confronted by God's awesome power.

Some of us simultaneously experienced many feelings: fear, wonder, happiness, unworthiness, joy, belief, disbelief, peace, etc.. As we continued to look, the center of the sun became totally white and looked like the Host. Carol and I could see a crown of thorns forming at the top.

I remembered that when I saw this phenomena the last time, I'd wished to see Jesus. No sooner had I finished that thought than the center of the sun turned into a television screen and I saw the face of Jesus: He wore the crown of thorns, but He didn't have a tortured face. I felt He was looking at me. It felt peaceful. I described it to the others. They hadn't seen Jesus, but we all praised and thanked Him.

We kept looking, sometimes kneeling, sometimes standing, praising and thanking God, Jesus, and Mary. We were totally filled with joy and excitement. The last time, I had experienced fear mixed with joy. This time I was more at peace. I was an old hand at these things. I was now the proud son of a Father who does wondrous things.

The phenomena didn't show any sign of stopping so I suggested we say a Rosary while we watched. I thought to myself, "What do we do with this?" You just can't turn it off and walk away, so we prayed the Glorious Mysteries of the Rosary, sometimes stopping to comment on what we were seeing. When we had finished, I knew somehow that it was time for us to continue on to church.

As we left I realized that we were standing in the exact spot where I had seen the miracle of the sun before. I recalled that the first vision was just as spectacular, although different. I will cherish all the gifts I have received, but seeing Our Lord will always remain the most special to me.

We proceeded towards the church filled with great joy. As we left the vineyards near the back of the church, we noticed that the fields behind and beside the church were filled with thousands of people. All were saying the Rosary while waiting for Our Lady's nightly apparition. There may have been as many as twenty thousand people. The church itself was filled to capacity, and the grounds around it were covered with pilgrims hearing the Mass over loudspeakers. There appeared to be over twenty priests from all over the world on the outdoor altar. (One night at Mass, the Gospel was read in five different languages.)

You wouldn't think that such a great number of people could remain orderly and peaceful, but they did. When we gave one another the sign of peace at Mass it was as if we were glowing. Receiving communion was extraordinary, we felt filled with peace.

When we heard all those people singing Our Lady's favorite song, "Glory, Glory, alleluia," it gave us chills. We put our arms around one another as we sang, choked with emotion.

We decided to walk back, with flashlights in hand, through the fields again rather than brave the speeding taxi cabs on Medjugorje's only road. Heading in the direction of our house, we noticed that the moon was pink and it illuminated the whole valley. "What a breathtaking end to a beautiful day," I thought. Our fearless leader Vince calculated our hike and pointed us in a direction. These calculations had to be adjusted from time to time as we found ourselves blockaded in certain places with bramble bushes or steep drops.

We approached a farmhouse and heard a dog barking. As we got closer to him he became more agitated. He was standing between us and our final destination. Vince and Carol suggested we walk around. Marie and I were inclined to negotiate with the dog. However, Vince's rationale won out. We tried walking around, but it was impossible to get through. We would have to go back into the fields and find another path. Marie and I again suggested approaching the dog.

As we walked back in that direction, a peasant woman heard all the noise and came out of the house. She turned on the light and motioned us to pass while she held the dog. We greeted her and thanked her as we walked by. I noticed that the dog was tied to a leash. The woman smiled warmly as we passed.

The villagers have such patience. Could you imagine the reception you would get in the States if you approached someone's house from the rear in the dark? The lady had such a generous and loving face. I walked back to her and gave her all my chocolate bars and then thanked her again.

After dinner, Marie, Carol, and Vince, along with others in our group decided they wanted to climb Mt. Krizevac (Cross Mountain). When they asked me, I was apprehensive, having disclosed to them before we left for Medjugorje, that I had a desire to climb the big mountain, but that I had a problem with vertigo. Not wanting to disappoint them, I reluctantly accepted, thinking that I shouldn't have had so much homemade wine at dinner.

They were so excited! Our first full day had been packed with so much wonder they didn't want it to end. It was around eleven o'clock. I had been up early and it had been a physically and emotionally taxing day. As we were waiting for everyone to gather, Penny asked us how our day had gone. We burst out with all the details, making special mention of the fact that we had looked into the sun for twenty full minutes.

Penny's face showed concern. She began to tell us of a conversation she had with Wayne Weibel earlier in the week. He received a letter from a pilgrim who had looked into the sun and damaged her eyes. He was going to include a statement of caution in his next newsletter. Apparently some people try to force the vision to happen.

Hearing this, my serenity began to wane. We were all disturbed by the news. We checked whether anyone was experiencing any difficulty with their vision. No one was, so we adopted a more comfortable composure. With the help of our explorer/dentist we concluded that we had witnessed the phenomena about five hours earlier and if damage had occurred we would have already been feeling bad effects.

I couldn't believe how easy it was for me and others to lose the serenity and peace of God. How we could have had such doubts, especially after witnessing what we had seen? It's incredible how the guy with the pitchfork can so subtly inject doubt and confusion into our lives and have such impact (Mt 14:18-31).

17

Krizevac and Healing

WE WALKED UP THE ROAD to the path and began our climb, led by a pilgrim who had climbed the hill earlier in the week. Bill Gavigan turned out to be an a surgeon from Nashville, (first we had a dentist, now a surgeon as leader.) As we climbed, my friends reassured me by remaining close to me. We had flashlights but there was really no need for them, the pink moonlight was so bright.

After climbing for about fifteen minutes, we came to a dead-end, with no visible path to follow. So much for our surgeon/explorer, we had lost our way! He decided to go exploring. Guess with whom? Vince! They disappeared into the night. After a while we called out to them, but we received no answer. Then we began discussing the way sound carried on mountain tops. All of us hoped that Bill and Vince hadn't gotten lost. The thought of having to search for them was not an appealing one. Eventually, the two returned, claiming that there was no outlet, and that we had to descend in order to find the right path. It was then I fully realized how far up we had climbed. You could see the tiny lights of the houses in the distant valley as we started down. Eventually we found our way and began to climb again. We prayed at each station of the cross. Father Lou had a book of the stations of the cross with him that had touching meditations.

As we proceeded further I started to feel the lightness of the air. It was thinning. Our breathing became heavy so we decided to stop for awhile. Up to this point I had been fine. Even though we were up high, the shrubbery along side the path seemed to provide a feeling of containment.

After resting a short time we continued upward. The path became steeper and I began having trouble whenever I looked down. When we arrived at the seventh station I couldn't go any further. The climb became too steep. Father Louis tried to encourage me by associating my climb to the passion of Jesus, the times Jesus fell while carrying the cross to Calvary. I really wanted in my heart to complete the climb, but I knew it was impossible. This was my best. Vince, being the special guy that he is suggested that we continue reading the stations, so that I could complete them with the group. The love and concern of these people was overwhelming.

I was disappointed and some of that old doubt filtered in. I began struggling inside, questioning my trust of God. Was I giving into fear? Was I accepting my limitations?

Vince, with great sacrifice, accompanied me down. I knew how much he wanted to reach the summit and I told him it wasn't necessary. Once I descended a little I'd be alright I tried to assure him. His concern was genuine and unselfish. He wouldn't leave me.

We descended the length of one station and I began to regain my equilibrium, noticing that we were in an area that had more foliage. As we got to the level of the second station, I tried to find my special garden. We looked and looked but just couldn't find it. I thought that praying there while we waited for the others to return would perhaps save the evening for Vince.

When we got back to the house we sat outside and talked. I tried to work through my embarrassment. Wanting to defend myself, I felt the need to explain to Vince the details of my physical problems (for example, a ruptured ear drum, degenerative arthritis in the neck, etc.) Childhood scenes came into my head. I heard those familiar lines: "...not good enough, not smart enough, not strong enough..." However, Our Lady's peace found its way back into my heart as I began to see my accomplishments. I made a mental inventory of all the milestones I had reached. This was an internal battle for me — positive combating of negative thoughts.

We had talked for quite awhile and became concerned about the others. We decided to walk up to the foot of the mountain path, looking for flashlights flickering and hoping to hear their voices. They finally came down and were surprised we had waited for them. We quickly found out that Carol had fallen and split her finger open. It was a bad cut.

Back at the house, we got to see our surgeon ply his real trade. He fixed Carol up with a butterfly bandage while we watched. Our doctor/explorer received an opportunity to redeem his image. You don't need skills in leading expeditions if you are talented in mending wounds.

I began to accept the fact of my physical disability, one that placed limitations on me while realizing I would never be a Mickey Mantle and hit fifty four home runs in a season, I was certainly gifted in many other ways. That evening I realized that all those fingers that pointed at me over the years had kept me not only from acknowledging my gifts, but also from accepting the reality of my handicaps. I learned that there is freedom in both.

Some day, I may attempt another climb up Mt. Krizevac because I'd like to see the cross and pray there, not because I need to prove anything. I now realize that if we accept our disabilities we are more predisposed to accept God's help. I see now that being me, with all my limitations, is exactly who the Lord called me to be. John Powell says in his book, *The Christian Vision:*

> *True appreciation of our personal uniqueness offers each of us the truth that sets us free from these endless and painful contests. God says to each of us: 'You are unique, the one and only you. I have loved with an eternal love. I do not get new ideas nor do I lose old ones; so the thought of you has always been in my mind. And the image of you has always had a special, warm place in my heart. You have been given an important role to play in my world. You have a unique message to deliver, a unique song to sing, a unique act of love to bestow. This message, this song, and this act of love have been entrusted exclusively to the one and only you.'*

The Feast of the Cross was coming up in a few days, and I planned to spend the day by myself because everyone would probably climb the mountain for the feast day celebration. However, I knew in my heart that the Lord would provide.

18

Vicka and Marija

GORDANA AND MARY WOKE US UP early the next day for an eight o'clock interview with Vicka at her home, which was also in Bijakovici not far from Ivan's house. I decided to walk there. It was a good distance, but I loved the peaceful atmosphere, and I also got a good perspective of the people and their way of life. When I arrived at Vicka's home, pilgrims were crowded in the street. Vince, Carol and Marie beckoned me toward them. Vince was making his way through the people, inching his way onto the crowded patio.

We found a great spot close to where Vicka stood on the exposed staircase. She smiled warmly and greeted everyone and, as is the custom with the visionaries, she led us in prayer. Had Mary and Gordana gotten their times mixed-up? The interpreter began translating her words into Italian.

Fortunately I could translate the main points for my traveling companions. We were very touched by Vicka's openness and patience. It's clear how much she loves people. By this time I had taken out my borrowed video camera, asking Vince for some tutoring on the machine. Together we got the camera working, and I was able to videotape most of the interview with Vicka. When you look at someone through the eye of a camera, you seem to concentrate more on them. Studying her face and mannerisms, Vicka comes across with great warmth, her inner beauty jumps out at you.

Vicka's message was similar to Ivan's, focusing heavily on the youth of today and the worldly pressures that they are under. She specifically mentioned drugs, sex, and abortion. She said that Our Lady was cautioning us to minister to our families and pray with our children each day. She reminded us again of God's love for us and the messages. The messages were asking us to pray the Rosary, attend Mass, receive communion and reconciliation. When the interview ended she graciously autographed prayer books for rememberance. We were joyful as we left her home.

Walking a short distance to Marjia's house, we found the street to be even more crowded. The Italian pilgrims that had left Vicka's house had made their way to Marjia's, too. However both groups were able to follow her words as she spoke in fluent Italian, and had an English language translator.

Marija appeared to be very conservative. She told people that taking pictures was unnecessary. She's more introverted than Vicka, expressing basically the same message but in a more serious posture.

I thought back to the interview with Ivan. A pilgrim had asked him if he was afraid of Our Lady. His response was that he was more afraid of us. Most of the visionaries are introverts. They must find it quite unsettling facing large crowds of people and answering a wide variety of questions. Many people who are trained for public speaking find it uncomfortable at times. However the visionaries all meet the challenge that God has given them with courage and prayer. Marija led us in prayer as she completed her talk.

We decided to climb Apparition Hill again that morning since it was close to Marija's house. Our prayers had a more serious tone to them as we climbed. The talks with the visionaries created a meditative spirit in me. The prayer experience on the summit was more solemn that morning. As we continued praying a little male dog walked passed us and went up and down the rocky path a couple of times. It didn't seem to beg for attention as dogs usually do. Then I heard a woman's voice say, "It's crying!" When I looked over, he was passing us again, this time with a dead puppy in his mouth. He just didn't know what to do with it. Finally he made his way up through the steep rocks and disappeared. Carol and I were standing together at this point, and were saddened by the sight. It was quite a contrast to the experiences we had there earlier in the week.

Afterward, we made our way through the crowd, down into the fields, towards church for Mass. It was a beautiful sunlit day, and after seeing the visionaries we were charged up. The visionaries share Our Lady's motherly advice in such a way that you know you're her child and God's.

After Mass we strolled leisurely up the road passing a small outdoor fruit stand. We decided to buy some fresh fruit. There was a wide variety so we each picked out what we liked and fantasized about having a smorgasbord for lunch. When we got back I volunteered to prepare the fruit. It was such a beautiful day I decided to set the table on the front patio which had a view overlooking the valley.

As I completed my work, Penny and another pilgrim she introduced as Bernie Kennedy stopped to admire the display of fruit. I invited them to join us, but Penny said she was fasting and suggested that Bernie, who was hungry, eat with us. He told me later that he was a Long Island supermarket entrepreneur. He asked me where I was from and where my wife and I did our grocery shopping. When he heard the name, he smiled and said that it was one of his stores. I complimented him on the store's quality and the service as we waited for the others to finish freshening up.

It was nice to see a man of wealth and worldly success seeking God. I hoped that he would carry Our Lady's message to those of his economic level. There is still so much work to do to deliver the message of Medjugorje. Those with worldly power can cover much ground with their influence. I thought of the Church, certainly it could have enormous impact. It is sometimes frustrating to think of how slowly the Church works before giving its blessing. With all the fruits that have been realized so far by the phenomena, it's hard to be patient while the Church remains cautious.

We ate when the gang eventually returned, and rehashed the events of the morning. We were like kids at a picnic. I'm sure the other pilgrims enjoyed seeing our child-like enthusiasm and I can honestly say that I have never known such happiness. Every little thing we did had so much meaning. It made me realize how completely delighted a soul could be in God's presence. If we can feel this good on earth, heaven has to be total bliss.

By simply letting go and enmeshing ourselves in Our Lady's plan we were receiving healing and peace. I remembered my first trip again. Although I had had challenges, all that I had endeavored to accomplish in my search for God had been realized. The gifts of discernment and understanding of oneself were part and parcel of the healing process, and as the song says, "Healing is just another word for love."

After the refreshing lunch, I continued to sit at the table waiting for the dynamic trio to freshen up again. While waiting, I was joined by Peg and Joe Carr and Mary Santagat, pilgrims in our group from the Cape Cod, Massachusetts area. We shared the experiences that we were having. Peg told me about her reasons for visiting Medjugorje. Apparently her grandson had been seriously ill and she and her husband were motivated to bring Our Lady their petition of healing for him. She also mentioned that she herself had been recovering from serious illness, and in the last three years had required three major operations for a diseased pancreas. Their faith was inspiring. She shared that she was able to climb Apparition hill, but while praying at the top she became quite ill. A severe nausea had overcome her and she had had to descend. When she got almost to the bottom of the hill, she had to throw up, feeling embarrassed and guilty doing that on holy ground. She said from that point on she has felt terrific and asked to be remembered in my prayers.

A few years ago, I had asked a friend of mine in my spiritual community to remember me in prayer and he had suggested we pray right then. Why wait? With that in mind I suggested to Peg and the others that we pray for her together. We joined hands, and I began to pray spontaneously, taking my left hand and placing it on the side of her head and I began asking the Lord for healing.

As I closed my eyes a picture of a human heart, with bright red color and a golden backdrop of fire appeared, at its top was a golden crown. I opened my eyes for a second and told the others what I saw. When I closed them again, I saw the crucifix as if it where animated with a golden burst of light behind it. We concluded our prayer with an Our Father, Hail Mary and a Glory Be. We all felt very peaceful and Peg shared that she had felt a penetrating heat coming from my hand.

Peg said that both Father Lou and Father Moyna had prayed separately over her for healing. She remembered Father Moyna's prayer: "Lord we believe that we can heal through you and that the power of healing was given to the disciples." It was a touching interlude. Our Lord was showing us clearly that we have to be involved with each other and that love is a healing instrument. He calls us to both empathy and compassion, to make ourselves one in Him.

The next scheduled stop for us that afternoon was to return to church for a talk by Father Jozo. Yes, Father Jozo! He was allowed to visit Medjugorje a few times a week to speak to pilgrims and say Mass. It's ironic! This was the same man who was falsely incarcerated by the communist government for a year and a half. When he was released he was not permitted to return to his parish. In a few short months since my first visit the government had capitulated to democracy. He continues to be an example to all of us, and exemplifies Scripture which tells us that "with God everything is possible" (Mk 10:27).

The church was extremely crowded but I was able to find a spot next to a pole right in front. It was fortunate that I was able to stand close to Father Jozo. He spoke in Italian with an English translator. You could feel the spirit of God within him. His words were truly inspired. He spoke of God and Our Lady with such great love that you realized you were in the presence of a truly holy man. As he continued his talk, what appeared to be a couple of bus loads of Italian pilgrims began to push their way through the already crowded church. Father Jozo was so deeply engrossed in the spirit as he spoke that he appeared startled by the distraction. He immediately admonished these over zealous people, and firmly informed them that there would be another talk in Italian after this one, and that they should wait without disturbing us.

It seems that Father Jozo has these distractions quite often. The guy with the pitchfork apparently works overtime to sabotage the delivery of his messages. These messages come from a person of such deep faith that he accepted intimidation and imprisonment rather than deny his God. We were thrilled when we left the church that night, just being in Father's presence was inspiring; he made God real for us.

Making our way to the main road, we hugged each other before separating. The others were going to climb Apparition Hill; I was scheduled to spend the evening with Jozo Kisilj, my friend and host. It was hard leaving them, but I knew they'd be in good company. Later, they told me there had been a magnificent sunset and after descending they had sat on the front steps of the guest house watching the bright sky in awe and gratitude.

—19—

Reunion: My Croation Family

BEFORE I LEFT from my first visit I had asked Jozo when would be a good time for me to return. He answered quickly, "September! The weather is good, Armando!" I learned in Medjugorje, to follow suggestions. One never knew when suggestions could turn into miracles. I remembered the stories my mother told about her homeland. Sicily is similar to Medjugorje and apparently has the same type climate and weather, complete with fig trees, grape vines and salamanders. I had hoped to visit Sicily on my way home and was disappointed that it didn't work out, but I felt secure that God was leading me. He knows what's good for me and when the time will be right.

On my last visit Jozo and Merissa had wanted me to show them how to cook Italian food, but we couldn't find the ingredients. I wasn't about to use the olive oil Father Jozo had blessed for me and canned tomatoes were nowhere to be found. However this time I remembered to bring a supply of ingredients with me. It had been no easy task carrying heavy cans of tomatoes and a half gallon of olive oil on a transatlantic journey. It's amazing how close Yugoslavia is to Italy and Spain, yet the standard of living can not support the purchase price of imported olive oil.

Merissa and I selected a day when we could prepare dinner together. She was especially happy that I had insisted Jozo help me cook. She and her sister Nevenka were giggling and repeatedly told me in broken English that, "Jozo no cook!" shaking their heads at the same time. The roles in this small village are still very defined. Men do men's work and women do men's and women's work. They were thrilled when they saw me and some of the other male pilgrims helping them clear the tables at night. They didn't understand it, but I know they liked it.

Because of the strict fasting they do on Wednesdays and Fridays, we had to schedule our afternoon Italian food festival on the same afternoon the group was scheduled to visit Father Jozo in Tihaljina. It was fortunate for me that I had already heard him speak at the church. I felt badly that I would be unable to go, but felt committed to spend time with these wonderful people. God is so very present in them. They do so much for all the visitors, working seven days a week, while at the same time caring for their families. I wanted to do something for them.

How big the children had gotten in just a few months! Ivana their oldest was now fourteen and attended school in Mostar. Mostar is a large city, a good hour's drive from Medjugorje through a mountain range with roads that border steep drops. Merissa beamed with pride as she told me about her grown-up daughter, who traveled by bus to school in the big city. How grateful I was to be with them again. I remembered how Jozo had cared for me in my time of distress when I lost my passport. Wanting to express my thanks to him, I invited him out for a relaxing dinner. He took me to a restaurant in the outskirts of Citluk. The last time we were there together I had been in a panic. This time we feasted on scampi (a local crayfish) which was quite good. We enjoyed ourselves, talking the night away. Our conversation moved from politics, to work, family, and children. However, God and morality remained the underlying issue in each topic. Jozo's spirituality amazed me. His relationship with the Lord is remarkable.

As he spoke, I thought to myself, how difficult it has been for us Christians in the modern world to find God. We approach Him with slide rule and graph paper as if He were a math problem. We have to read all the latest books, attend Christian renewals, seminars and retreats, while stockpiling videos and audio cassettes prepared by prophetic teachers, all in search of Him. We need to be constantly reminded to "stop and smell the roses." These people, in contrast, could be seen as flowers themselves, growing where they were planted, one with their environment and nurtured by God.

Mother Angelica once said on television, "Stop 'trying' to believe and believe!" There's no question in Jozo's or Merissa's minds about the existence of God. For them it's a simple truth. When asked if he believed, Carl Jung the noted psychiatrist once said, "I don't believe, I know."

Jozo and Merissa know. Their insight comes from a life of being what God gifted them to be, basically satisfied, and committed to His will. Our Lady made no mistake in choosing Medjugorje. The spiritual soil is firm and fertile.

When we returned to Medjugorje late that evening, Jozo took me to his cousin's new Pizzeria-coffee bar. We had a few espressos and I noticed how much they supported each other. They were part of each other's life. Walking in the human condition together, passing time the same way their ancestors did. They are one with themselves, their community and their God, showing a confidence and security that only comes from old established relationships.

Joan and I listen to our daughters. Our two oldest are expecting children of their own. We get a kick out of hearing about all the modern concepts surrounding childbirth today. Biophysical tests, sonagrams and parental bonding techniques, to name a few. We marvel at their generation. This generation finds it necessary to see the baby on a television screen before it's born. They must know its sex ahead of time so they can paint the room the right color. They rehearse their first meeting to insure proper bonding. Guess what? They're still going to have to get up in the middle of the night and experience some good old-fashioned bonding.

We had a lot of fun later on in the week cooking that traditional meatball and spaghetti dinner. Jozo reluctantly helped me chop onions and prepare the tomato sauce. The facial expressions and giggles from Merissa and Nevenka proved to be too much for him. Cooking, for him, was like trying to thread a needle with boxing gloves on. I had to complete the job.

Matthew, their nine-year-old son, waited patiently to test a fried meatball. I remembered the ritual from my youth. As she cooked Sunday dinner, my mom would ask me to "taste" (an official position) the meatballs in case they needed more seasoning. This was the same ploy I used with my girls as they grew up. Matthew was now being introduced to one of my own family traditions— meatball tasting. Of course, he gave his expert opinion without any coaxing, "Good, Good, Armando! I even like that, even no sauce."

Merissa and Nevenka watched me working. They looked at me as if I were a U.F.O. For them it was probably like experiencing a minor miracle, not only seeing a man in the kitchen, but one producing palatable food.

That wonderful dinner together will never be forgotten. They invited the whole family, including grandparents and cousins. Nevenka remarked, as she bit into a meatball, "Oh! Armando," shaking her head in approval, unable to verbalize her pleasure in English. It reminded me of the sounds my wife Joan makes when she eats my pasta pezelle (macaroni with peas). It was gratifying to see their smiles and heads nodding, expressing a simple childlike joy. It was for me a sight as uplifting and powerful as seeing the sun spin. They made me feel like family, sharing their unity and covenant with God. When love is expressed, God is present.

Thanking the Lord, I prayed my Rosary while walking to church that afternoon. He had shown Himself to me again, this time in the form of a loving embrace through His Croation children. I thought back to how beautifully the day began. Vince suggested we try and find my garden on Mt. Krizevac. After breakfast the four of us hiked up the road to the path. The location seemed to elude me again, but after a few tries I found the entryway. It had been covered up with a small fallen tree. As we entered we could feel the peace. I pointed to the rock I had sat on while praying the Rosary. The terraced enclosure appeared to be much larger than in my memory.

My companions were thrilled by its intimate seclusion. We decided to climb up through the rocks to another flattened level. We sat together on large stones which were nestled together, looking over the garden-like terrace into the valley. We were all filled with excitement as we began praying the Rosary. It seemed that the more we prayed, the more peaceful we became. We were experiencing another close moment together. After completing the fifteen decades of the Rosary, we sang Our Lady's song, "Glory, Glory, Alleluia," A gust of wind made its way through the garden as if caressing us. Because it was very still that day it seemed to come out of nowhere. We all knew without saying that Our Lady was present. We were so happy, giggling and acting like little children as we hugged and took pictures of one another. Even now, I long to be in that garden, in the security of Our Lady's embrace. I had come a long way spiritually since first praying there and I recognized the effects of my healing.

It was a great send off for the others. They were on their way to Father Jozo's church in Tihaljina, about an hour drive from Medjugorje. I found out later that they had experienced the

Lord's healing embrace through Father Jozo's hands. Apparently after his talk, Father laid hands on people in the group and many "rested in the spirit."

They were warned that some people had a tendency to get up and run out of the church after the laying on of hands, but he told them that they should not worry or resist. Bob Nochta, a pilgrim from New Jersey sent me a copy of his journal in which he recounted how the events of that morning had touched him. Never having had that experience before, he prayed that the Holy Spirit would touch him. When Father Jozo laid his hands on him he 'went down and out,' to use his words.

In his journal Bob explained that there was a yellow and orange flash in front of his eyes, like a television going blank, and before he knew it, he was lying comfortably on the floor. He was fully aware of his surroundings, feeling a weight like a sheet of glass holding him down. He was unable to rise. He remembered being told about the urge to run when he entered the church but he felt he couldn't have gotten up even if he wanted to. After having this close encounter with the Holy Spirit he was deeply shaken and it took some time to compose himself.

My pilgrim friends told me how Father Jozo spoke with such great love. Bob also took notes while Father gave his talk. As I read them they inspired me with their profound meaning and spiritual direction. The essence of what Bob heard and recorded is:

> *Go back and set your families free from bondage. There is no love, no faith without prayer. The world can be changed through prayer. Jesus is a sign of our faith and He has signs along our path, the sacraments. You won't get lost if you follow these signs. Pray! Fast! Don't be afraid to fast and sacrifice. Ask the Lord to purify you from your ego and*

remove all your masks. Inner freedom comes through sacrifice and because you love Jesus, the Blessed Mother and the Eucharist! How will you know unless through this sacrifice. We love through our sacrifice. Love, joy, enthusiasm and freedom come through sacrifice. You receive a freedom that wouldn't allow the police to stop you from coming here. Thousands upon thousands of pilgrims have come to confess their sins and to ask for penance. Years ago it was a Church with trees and a priest under each branch. Today with restaurants, shops, and hotels. But still the 'Prodigal Sons' return. A most inspiring parable, all of us are he who returns here. Our Father welcomes us back. Confess every month, go to the Father regularly and He will clothe you with joy! Don't be afraid to pray for your confessor. See the goodness and love of God who does not forsake us. Mother Mary asks us to pray for priests. When she was asked about priests it was the first time tears were seen in her eyes. Pray for priests! Our Lady said, "Say to my beloved sons (priests): 'love my people, have confession for my church, pray for my priests, start to pray for them.'" In a flower of prayer there is no room for Satan, each person praying daily for a different petal in a flower, with the priest in the center.

Pick a different petal for each day and pray for that priest. Priests need your prayers to be capable of preaching. Don't leave them out of your hearts. Don't criticize. We know our weaknesses. Let your hearts be open to us so we can hear your confession, so we can give you the sacraments. The word of God to you is the Eucharist; it is so important to respect the living body of Christ that is here. The eternal light burns next to it. Moses received the light into his heart. Jesus lit the light again at the last supper. It is the eternal life! Mary cries when speaking about the Eucharist. Kneel before the Tabernacle in silence. We should respect all life, all creatures. This light is the great encounter between us and God. Rediscover the light of the Eucharist here in Medjugorje. Make the light of the Tabernacle in your own church the light of Jesus in your heart. All light, all love comes from Jesus. The drop of water added to the wine is the symbol of us mixing with Jesus, coming together with Him in union through His precious blood. You become more precious and holy in the eyes of God through the Eucharist. Focus on the altar and become one with Jesus. Our Lady says: "Let the Eucharist be your life. Let your life become the Eucharist."

We've forgotten the Bible. This makes Our Lady sad. It's not just a book, it's the word of God! Even the enemies of Jesus said: "No one has spoken like Him or written a word like Him." It is unjust to call the word of God a book. Parents are called to be the first ones to proclaim the word of God! Do so!

Put the Bible on one side and the mass media on the other. Our Lady calls us to this. We must do this. We owe this to God! Set the Bible free. Open it every day and read it. We don't know the face of the one true God! That is why Mary wants to make you a prophet by your pilgrimage to Medjugorje. We must obey Our Blessed Mother so that Jesus can be present in our time! Mary says we are important for the whole world, for God!

Let me share one more thing from my heart. When you arrive at home build a family altar because every family is a church, a place where we gather together. Place your crucifix on the altar. Jesus crucified is the greatest teacher who will teach and forgive, a sacrifice of one for all. Place the image of Mary below the cross. Behold your mother, her values, her virtues, her image on one side, her word on the other. Place your rosary on your altar. Pray every day. This is your weapon to conquer Satan, like David who slew Goliath with five stones (five decades). Kiss your Bible daily, grab it when you get home and feel the divine seed of the love of God! You can change the face of your life. Place holy water on the altar to bless your home. When the visionaries first sprinkled Holy Water on the Blessed Mother and said, "If you are Satan go away from us," Mary said, "Be not afraid, it is me. I'm watching over your families." By this you will know that this altar is the place for your family to encounter God's love. Praise God!

It was a touching experience and they were deeply moved by Father Jozo. To top off the afternoon, he permitted Father Lou to say Mass for the group in his private chapel and when they left they saw the sun dancing in the parking lot.

20

Slaying Dragons

ARRIVING EARLY for the scheduled talk that morning, I decided to sit and relax on a bench by the side door of the church. As I sat and prayed my Rosary, a tall, robust gentlemen in his late fifties or early sixties sat down next to me. Before long we began to talk with each other. He told me he was a Franciscan priest, Father Winfreid De Mersman, originally from Belgium, who for the last forty years had lived and worked as a missionary in Zaire (Belgium Congo) at the Mission St. Bavon. He had worked at the mission without a church and as the only priest for most of his career. While visiting Medjugorje, he met the pastor of the church of St. James, through this acquaintance he was given funds to erect a church. His parish has about one hundred and fifty thousand parishoners, and he now ministers the sacraments with the assistance of one or two native-born priests. As he spoke I thought this is one more of the many fruits being harvested through Our Lady's presence in Medjugorje. We exchanged names as we left and he went to prepare to concelebrate Mass. As he walked away I felt in awe of him. His simplicity and humility were quite inspirational. How many of us could trust God that way, to give up our personal needs and wants and live as he did all those years?

As I continued to sit there meditating on my chance meeting with Father, I notice a panhandler moving from person to person on the church plaza, shaking pilgrims down for money. I overheard him telling people in broken English how he had become stranded after losing his wallet. He claimed that he had no money to purchase a return ticket to Italy. I shook my head as I watched, thinking how his tactics were no different than those employed by hustlers on Times Square in New York.

He eventually made his way to me, using the same approach as he did with the others. I responded to him in Italian, which surprised him and suggested that he visit the rectory and ask the Franciscans for help. He said, as he made an impatient gesture with his hand, "Everybody says the same thing." He asked me where my Italian roots originated from. I told him I was of Sicilian ancestry. Upon hearing this he gestured again, in a classic Italian mannerism, by raising and rotating his hand. He had a smile on his face, as if to say, "You can't fool Sicilians, they wrote the book!" He waved goodbye and walked back to the center of the plaza and joined two friends in conversation. They were probably comparing their takes. A short time later a woman in her late thirties, who appeared to be an American pilgrim, stopped to offer him a few dollars. Taking him aside, she apparently began explaining to him about the efforts she had made to collect money on his behalf. I had the urge to warn her, but remembered where I was. There were no accidents here, I thought.

Our Lady is on the case. She would somehow use this experience to enlighten both of them. I was confident that some lesson or healing would come out of it. I felt sad for them, one with no respect for others, taking whatever he could, and the other with diminished self-esteem eager to give, to gain acceptance of others, at any cost.

It was quite a contrast for me. Within minutes I had met two entirely different people, a devout missionary priest and a con-artist, both of whom were drawn to the same place for very different reasons. One coming in faith to nourish himself and others spiritually, the other to prey on charitable hearts and feather his nest at their expense.

After the talk I walked back toward the main road and met Father Jim. We decided to have coffee at one of the open air bars. It seems that whenever loneliness hits me the Lord always provides me with company.

As we sipped our espresso, Father confided to me that he was a recovering alcoholic. I couldn't believe the way he came out with it. We hadn't even stirred the coffee and he blurted out, "I'm an alcoholic." My son-in-law did the same thing to me when we met for the first time. It went: "Hello Sir, it's nice to meet you. I'm a recovering alcoholic."

My initial response usually is to say, "I'm a compulsive overeater!" We all can take something out of the bundle we carry around with us. There must be a need in us to share our secrets and still be accepted for who we are, scars and all.

Father went on to describe the turmoil he experienced coming to terms with this disease. He explained how he suffered and caused pain to others because of it. I immediately felt close to him. There is no greater gift than sharing oneself. His struggle was no different then anyone else's. We are all in our own way fighting dragons, some struggles are simply more obvious then others.

It was hard for him to share his difficulty. Priests are expected to be perfect and trained to be distant when it comes to personal matters. He courageously decided to inform his parishioners and admitted his struggle to them during the Sunday Masses. He was gratified and relieved with their loving response. I wasn't surprised to hear this. Most of us are wounded one way or another in life. Struggles are commonplace. By his confession he became a witness and an example of hope. It is only by admitting our powerlessness that we find and turn to God. Our God works through people (2Co1:9-10). Realizing how special he was, I began to feel guilty for all my criticism of priests. I had had a penchant for pointing out their imperfections.

They had to be perfect because I couldn't be. They had the responsibility to see me through to heaven. If they were human, who could I lean on? When we suffer from low self-esteem we create idols. If we don't view ourselves as being capable, we need to depend on others. The ironic part about that is that we usually are stronger than our idols. Those who accept that role are usually more insecure, needing more control and power, and usually they are less interested in a relationship with God.

If we face the truth, like Father did, we can build on the foundation of the gifts that God gave to each of us (Jas 1:17). The primary gift is God's infinite love. Just think about it! If we truly believe that God loves us unconditionally, would we suffer from self-esteem problems? Just look at the magnitude of the Medjugorje phenomena — the conversions, the rejuvenation of prayer, fasting and reconciliation seen throughout the world. Atheistic communism in eastern block countries is self-destructing. The United Nations is finally working together to protect the sovereignty of helpless nations and fight for human rights.

God loves us so much that He's practically hitting us on the head with a two-by-four of love at Medjugorje. He calls us to him with all of our imperfections. He provides the world with exceptional graces. We need only have eyes to see and ears to hear (Acts 28:27).

We need to begin seeing our true selves with courage like Father did. Hi, I get angry! Hi, I'm selfish at times. Hi, we're America and we're broke." When these things are hidden and ignored they own us. When we acknowledge them before God what we have left is the gift God made us to be.

Father's ministry today is rich with compassion and empathy. His experience can touch others because he knows their pain intimately. To me there's no greater power than reaching out to others with compassion. Compassion wins souls. Compassion feels another's pain, forgives his imperfections and rejoices in his gifts. Father was a gift to me that day, a true "wounded healer."

My discussion with Father was no accident. I gained insight into my own limitations and ministry and realized that when we tell the world who we are, we don't have to cover up who we are not.

We returned to church for the Rosary and later walked back home after Mass. We had created a bond. Even though I didn't get to see Father Jozo that day, Our Lady provided me with a special new friend and continued inner healing.

21

Happy Birthday Mary

DINNER THAT EVENING was quite lively. We shared the exciting events of our day as we ate. Our experiences were powerful in different ways. I had another first that night, when we finished our meal. One of the pilgrims, Jose, kept talking about having a scapular ceremony all week. He brought a supply of scapulars (see glossary) with him from the states for that purpose, giving the impression that he was driven to accomplish this, so we arranged for the ritual that evening.

Just as we finished dinner, Vince and Terry Talbet, pilgrims from Scottsdale, Arizona stopped to visit. They were on an extended business trip, traveling through Europe by car. Vince is an investment banker. We met on the road in front of Jozo's house. They spotted my Yankee baseball cap and heard me speak English as they were driving by and stopped to chat. They told me that they were alone so I invited them to stop in and visit with our group in the evening. They couldn't have arrived at a better time as the ceremony was about to begin. It's like Our

Lady had given them a personal invitation.

Father Jim and Father Lou presented the scapulars to us by placing them around our necks while they recited a prayer. After the touching ceremony, we had another surprise. Apparently Father Lou, when returning with the others from Father Jozo's, asked the bus driver to stop in a town so he could purchase a birthday cake for Our Lady. September 8 has been used as her birthdate by the church for centuries. However, Mary told the Visionaries at the apparition on August 5 that this date was her real birthday. (The children had asked her why she was dressed so special that day.) Maybe when the church finally approves the apparitions we will celebrate the August 5 date. In the meantime I'm sure she won't disapprove of two birthday celebrations. So, Merissa provided us with a candle and joined our festivities.

Father placed the candle in the cake and as he lit it we began to sing "Happy Birthday" to our heavenly Mother. It was a very moving experience. I felt as if she were there among us. Then we sang her song again, "Glory! Glory! Alleluia!" Afterward, we joined hands in prayer, making a circle around the dining room and prayed the Hail Mary. We had a spontaneous offering up of prayer while continuing to hold hands. We prayed for world peace, our friends and families back home, the priests, the visionaries, and the people of Medjugorje.

While we were still standing in the circle with our hands clasped together, the episode of the dog on the hill popped into my head. I realized that it was a message. It represented the knowledge of God's pain and how frantic He is about all the children who are aborted. Like the dog, He was crying as any parent would at the loss of an offspring. I thought of the frustration He must feel with us. He loves each and every one of us. God is so deeply involved in our pain. The loss of any one of us gives Him great sorrow. I asked Father Jim to lead us in a prayer for the unborn. He found such beautiful words that it was apparent the plight of those deprived children had troubled him for a long time. Until that evening, I really hadn't related deeply to the issue of abortion. That was for people who were motivated for that ministry. My buddy Frank Lawrence, a member of my weekly group, had shared many times about his involvement. He would tell us about the rescue missions and protests he participated in. Even when he related the way a passerby would curse or criticize him and the other protestors, it still hadn't touched my heart.

Not until that evening did I relate the plight of the unborn to God's love. When we had been up on the hill that day I remembered thinking that it was unusual that we didn't experience any phenomena. The visit took on a serious tone, we prayed and were at peace, but the exciting impact of the other visits was missing. God was apparently asking us to take a look at ourselves, to become more introspective about the world we have made. Abortion has to be the ultimate rejection of God and His gifts. If those who participate in terminating human life only knew how much it hurt God and what impact it has on their souls, they would never permit it to happen.

The solidarity we shared that evening was inspiring. We were one with each other, a true community of believers, comfortable and happy. Although we came from different cultures and places, there were no barriers. We were one in the spirit.

After leaving the dining room, Marie and I decided to sit outside and look at the stars. As we sat it seemed that the clouds were quickly flowing by. Some of them appeared to have shapes. One was in the form of an angel playing a trumpet.

Jozo came by and I walked into the road with him while we talked. I remembered a dream I had had a couple of nights after I returned home from Medjugorje the first time. Jozo and I were standing in the dining room looking out at the sky over the valley in front of the guest house. While I was traveling back to Medjugorje I thought the dream might signify that something disturbing might happen. The memory of the dream had a heavy impact on me even though I couldn't remember all the details. What I finally realized was the dream was saying I was going to visit and see my friend again.

22

Feast of the Triumph of the Cross

THE NEXT MORNING I AWOKE in time to make eight o'clock Mass. The night before, the priest at church told us there would be only two Masses the following day on the Feast of the Triumphant Cross. One was scheduled at eight in the morning and the other at eleven atop Mount Krizevac.

Walking down to church was difficult for me that morning, I felt very alone, while I made my way through the crowd. The pilgrims were walking in the opposite direction towards the mountain, making their way to the footpath at the base. I was disappointed that I wouldn't be able to attend Mass there and celebrate the feast day in prayer at the foot of that mighty cross.

Mass was not the same for me that morning. My mind kept drifting back to my failed attempt of climbing the big mountain. I was feeling down on myself and realized how difficult old habits are to break. Continuing up the road towards the guest house, I found myself in the midst of many pilgrims, who even at that time, were making their way towards the mountain. There were groups of people saying the Rosary, while others were singing.

Now and then you could see groups of people passing with church banners and Yugoslav flags. The sidewalk restaurants were bustling with patrons. Some establishments had already begun to roast entire lambs in outdoor barbeque pits.

I decided to have breakfast, stopping at a place where I noticed people ordering barbequed sausages. The sauguages came with chopped raw onion and a small loaf of bread. It was probably a holiday specialty. Sitting at an outdoor table waiting for my order, I observed large numbers of people marching up the hill. It was inspiring to see so many devout followers of Jesus, committed and anxious to show their love by making the sacrifice of the steep climb.

Then I began to see a contrast. There was a noticeable element of commercialism here. I'm sure that some of the merchants were motivated only by money, but that wouldn't effect or discourage the visitors. They were here because of an internal call, driven by their search for God. I'm convinced that if you open your heart to God all your attention remains focused on a relationship with Him. It's the same as when young people fall in love—nothing distracts them from each other.

There were so many people now in the restaurant that they were having difficulty getting the food served. I reminded the waiter of my order by waving to him and continued to sit there praying the Rosary while I waited. A young man who was obviously drunk staggered up the street and sat uninvited at a table with three other young people. He ordered a drink and began shouting and clowning in Croation, acting out. The people there seemed to think it was amusing, almost encouraging him by their laughter. To me it was a sad sight, seeing someone that early drunk in the morning, barely able to stand on his feet, in such holy surroundings, was disturbing. I thought to myself that as close as the young man was to a life of peace filled with natural highs, he still couldn't see it. His experience of Medjugorje was a lot different from that of mine and many other pilgrims.

When you walk the fields, climb mountains and visit church all day, you become oblivious to the fast track of the world around you. It's inevitable that even this blessed little village will succumb to some degree to materialism and the attractions of the world. Hopefully when the politics are straightened out responsible business people will work with the Church towards keeping the area civilized.

The sausages were finally served and they were delicious, another first for me in Medjugorje! After paying the check, I started walking up the road and noticed an awning that said "Pizza Miki." I stopped in to see if Miki remembered our train ride together, but unfortunately he wasn't there.

When I got back to the house I was surprised to see Carol, Vince and Marie sitting in the dining room eating a late breakfast. Vince explained that they had slept late because they had decided to climb the mountain after we had retired for the evening the night before. They returned to the mountain at three-thirty in the morning.

I was elated that I wasn't going to spend the day alone after all. We decided to go to Apparition Hill that afternoon. It turned out that many of the people in our group did not venture up the big mountain that day either. A group of us walked the back road to the hill. Everywhere we went we prayed our Rosary together. It amazed me how compatible we were. When we got to the top of the hill you could see the many thousands of people on the crest of Mt. Krizevac across the valley. After a while we heard them singing. It was awesome! We also heard a strange sounding singing at times, almost as if it were lamenting. It was like the deep groaning of many people. It could have been just the way the sound carried from such a distance.

Unfortunately, Carol's migraine flared up again and she decided to go back to the guest house. Her husband, Vince, said he would go back with her but she said she would be alright. In Mejugorje I learned not to insist but to just let things happen and accept the turn of events. It turned out that the walk back for Carol had surprises for her. She said that while she walked in pain she felt lonely and called out to Jesus for help.

She said that she almost immediately experienced His presence, feeling a sensation, as if His arm was brushing against hers, as if He were walking with her and she became tranquil. It made her think of the story of the "Footprints in the Sand":

> *... The Lord replied, "My precious, precious child, I love you and would never leave you. During your times of trial and suffering, when you saw only one set of footprints, it was then that I carried you."*

The three of us continued praying for a while, then descended the hill and made our way back to town. We were thirsty and wanted to browse again in the Franciscan shop. After purchasing more rosaries and other items, we proceeded up the road to Jozo and Merissa's place. About halfway there we ran into Carol, who after resting became hungry and started down to town looking for us. After a short discussion, Vince and Carol decided to go for a pizza and went back down the hill. Marie and I headed back to the house to rest. We both felt that Carol and Vince needed some time alone together.

23

Matija, Marie, Miracles and Me

I ASKED MERISSA if we could pick some figs off the tree. She told me she would have Jozo show me where their fig trees were in the vineyards. "Armando, Jozo take you," she said. The next day Jozo commandeered little Matija (Matthew) into service. "Take Armando to fig trees, " he told him. I got the impression that Matthew had other plans and questioned his father in Croation. However, his minor protest was short-lived. He obeyed his dad with genuine respect and led Marie and me into the fields with enthusiasm. As we followed Matija we marveled at his sense of humor and personality. He loves to boast and has the confidence of a forty year old. He was leading us to "his" grapevines and "his" fig trees. "This is my land, Armando! Those are my fig trees," he said singling out three in a cluster of five.

The night before, during a conversation with his dad, Jozo claimed that this land had belonged to his family for over six hundred years. He explained that he and another villager who shares his name, had traced their family trees and suspected a family split around that time because of illegitimacy. In any case, they consider themselves cousins.

It's no wonder that little Matthew had such confidence and pride in "his land." He knew exactly where the property was without the benefit of boundary markers or fences. Marie and I were really taken by him. He has a charm and self-respect that could only come from a strong, loving family. He showed us the same generosity and openness as his parents. He graciously picked a handful of figs for us and while we ate he waited patiently for us to release him so he could join his friends.

What could be better than this? Here we were standing in this breathtaking valley, eating fresh figs off the trees, cognizant of how our heavenly Father provides for us. It amazed me of how much we take for granted.

Jozo explained to me when we were discussing the figs, that the fig trees grow wild. They were provided by nature and that anyone was free to pick their fruit and eat. However, the grapes were another story. They are grown through hard work and toil, and permission was needed before taking them. Everything seems to be so well-ordered and disciplined in the lives of these people. They've built a confidence that only comes from living with discipline and good moral choices. It was no accident that Matthew was assigned to accompany us. Marie and I needed to witness his confidence and self-esteem. It was a beacon of light for both of us. These important virtues were elusive to us for most of our lives.

Marie and I shared a great deal that afternoon. She admitted the extent to which she suffered due to low self-esteem. She explained how it had detrimentally affected her ability to sustain lasting relationships. It became clear to me why she had elected to visit Medjugorje. She needed to feel connected and important. Her pilgrimage was an admission of the hopelessness she felt. It was the gesture of a child turning to God with extended arms shouting: "Daddy! Daddy! Help me!"

I drifted a few steps from Marie, soaking up the panoramic view and feeling the peace of the moment. When I looked back toward Marie she had dropped to her knees in prayer. Overtaken by her childlike simplicity I was choked with tears. You could see the beauty and innocence of a child in her. She had opened her heart to God, and his child surrendered her brokenness and claimed her inheritance.

This brought to mind the gospel message of the unfruitful fig tree. Jesus tells us about a man who had a fig tree growing in his vineyard. When he looked for figs he never found any. He then told his gardener that he looked for figs on that tree for three years without success and instructed him to cut it down. "Why should it go on using up the soil?" he asked. The gardener responded, "Leave it alone, sir, for just one more year. I will dig around it and put in some fertilizer. If the tree bears fruit next year, so much the better, if not, then you can have it cut down" (Lk 13:6-9).

The gospel message made me think of myself and Marie. I remembered the spiritual cultivation we received from God that day in the vineyard. God is our patient gardener, encouraging us to grow through faith, the grace which is His fertilizer. Medjugorje can be viewed as a model greenhouse, showing the world through the visionaries and pilgrims how God nurtures us when we respond to His call.

It seemed as we walked toward the cemetery that day that many issues were surfacing. I found myself in the position of the "wounded healer," being utilized as an instrument of the Lord's gentle cultivation, offering insight and empathy into Marie's turmoil, because of a similar background of tribulation in my own life. As we approached the cemetery, I suggested we sit for awhile on one of the crypts and watch the sunset. As we climbed the stairs I noticed that a large grave had recently been excavated. Normally it would have troubled me to sit so close to the reality of death. I would have fantasized a skeletal hand reaching out and pulling me into the darkness.

Hollywood has done us a disservice about death. Fortunately for me now, the concept of death does not grip me with fear as it once did. I noticed how I'd grown since my first visit to Medjugorje, learning to accept death's inevitability. There is no question now in my mind about God's existence and His love. Death now promises me enlightenment and peace, not darkness.

Coincidentally, we sat on the same tombstone the young couple had used while watching the sunset, drinking wine and contemplating love. I recalled how I couldn't believe they hadn't seen the sun spinning then. They were so engrossed in the things of this world that it had obstructed their vision.

We continued to talk as the sun set, finding ourselves comfortable and at peace. It was a time of healing for her and affirmation for me. As she spoke, the darkened horizon seemed to be encircled by what appeared to be cathedral-like windows. The inner portion had a lighter-colored sky than the outer portion. Also, bursts of light flashed behind the mountains, like lightening. Yet the night sky was perfectly clear with bright stars. I remembered blinking my eyes, thinking that they were tired or wind-burned from being out all day, but the vision did not disappear. Marie and I were so engrossed in conversation that I didn't mention the incident to her. She was unburdening herself of many past hurts and needed a sympathetic ear.

The message coming through to me was that we needed to continue the purging process throughout our lives, seeking wholeness of body, mind, and spirit. Miracles are encouragement and kisses from heaven, but we need to strive for personal freedom and come to terms with our own free will. Vincent Rush in his book *"The Responsible Christian"* tells us:

> ***A major task in life for each of us, consequent-***

> *ly, is that we must work to achieve freedom in whatever aspect of life we are not free. It hardly needs to be said that no one of us is completely and perfectly free. What is said here is being said in an attempt to clarify the goal - so that, even if it takes each of us most of our individual lives to reach the goal, we will, at least, not give up. Becoming free is a life long process that saints achieve - but, then, sanctity is everyone's goal. It is important that we be both patient with ourselves in the struggle, and persevering in the effort - always mindful that we are not alone. "Ask and you shall receive.*

Rush also tells us:

> *One final word on promoting freedom needs to be added. If there is no freedom, there is no point in discussing and preaching Christianity. Jesus said, "I am the truth" (Jn 14:6) and we know too that the truth will make you free" (Jn 8:33).*
>
> *Too often Christians with the best of intentions decide they will take away people's freedom in order to keep them free from sin. Somebody once said, "The world is divided into two kinds of people - those who divide the world into two kinds of people and those who don't ... those who think the greatest evil in the world is sin, and those who think the greatest evil in the world is lack of freedom."*

A few days later some pilgrims told me that around the time of Our Lady's apparition a light similar to the one I saw while talking to Marie in the cemetery, had appeared inside the church above the altar. It was described to me as looking like a laser beam. Others claimed to have seen the face of Christ in the tabernacle.

We walked through the valley towards the church, feeling unburdened. It amazed me how I could sit in a cemetery, in darkness, on a tombstone, without the slightest bit of discomfort, about six feet from an open grave, and still feel so relaxed and peaceful.

Mass was just beginning as we positioned ourselves behind the large congregation in the field at the back of the church. The Gospel was read in about five languages again. We were standing next to two young Croation men. They were so enthusiastic about Mass.

It is unusual to see such devout young people. Most young people today have become so materialistic that they have adopted the identity of the "consumer," measuring themselves by what they have and how much they can get, rather than by who they are and how they can give.

When we offered each other the sign of peace the young men seemed to light up. I put my arm around one fellow while we sang Our Lady's song ("Glory, Glory, Alleluia"). He was teary-eyed as he placed his arm around my shoulder in return, and around his companion's shoulder. Marie moved in between them and we sang together, filled with enormous joy. After Mass we said goodbye. Before we left, the young man complimented me, saying to Marie while pointing to me, "Good man! Good man!" I was again choked with emotion.

24

Saying Goodbye

THROUGHOUT THE WEEK I THOUGHT of extending my stay in Medjugorje. The reality of eventually having to leave its peace was disturbing for me. This prompted me to suggest an alternate plan to the group, one which would allow us to stay as long as possible. The idea was that we could leave directly for the airport around two in the morning and arrive in Dubrovnik in time for our seven a.m. departure flight, thinking that we could always sleep on the plane.

However, I failed in this attempt to be a pilgrim/travel agent, and accepted that I was alone in my interest. Father Jim's explanation was reasonable. He felt that we needed a time for transition, to bridge the world we visited, with the one in which we live.

The night before we left I stayed up late packing. Mary Fistler had given me an empty suitcase and travel bag to take back with me. Apparently, she was having difficulty getting packages that her friends and family were sending her. She asked me to discuss this problem with the tour operator on Long Island and suggest to them that they repack her belongings into her luggage, making it easier for transport. The thought dawned on me, how lonely Mary must get at times, a young woman living detached from her family and the conveniences she enjoyed in the states. She is a true missionary, sacrificing her personal life to minister to the Lord in a foreign land. Her love for God is clearly visible when you look into her beautiful eyes. They mirror the presence of the Holy Spirit within her.

Those suitcases came in handy. I needed the space to carry all the religious articles I had purchased for friends back home, statues, pictures, rosaries, etc. I never would have had room for the beautiful crystal wine bottle and glass set that Jozo and Merissa had surprised me with earlier in the day. Again I had been choked with emotion while hugging and telling them that they themselves were the biggest gift of all for me. I also felt badly that they had spent so much money.

As I completed packing, Vince stopped by to suggest that we visit Apparition Hill in the morning for one last time before we left for Mass. They wanted to purchase a couple of articles and have them blessed after Mass before we left.

We took a taxi that morning to the foot of the hill because our time was limited. Even at that early time of day, there were many pilgrims negotiating the hill. We climbed while saying our Rosary again. When we got to the top, we were overwhelmed with a profound sense of peace. The valley below had become a familiar view, as if it were home. Being so close to God made everyone and everything in the world look and feel familiar and connected. The restrictions of our human form were momentarily lifted, giving us a glimpse of the world to come. A world which I now envision as being complete, and without any sense of longing.

Glancing up to the small cross Vince and I erected the day before, I quickly realized the honor God showed, allowing us to make our mark on such holy ground. He really loves us and He has called us, through Our Lady. We are graced!

We were glowing inside as we descended. The pace of the rosary was accelerated so that we could accomplish everything we had planned to do before we left. While Vince, Carol and Marie browsed in the shops at the foot of the hill, I was busy taking pictures. I spotted two goats grazing off to the side of the path leading up the mountain. I marveled at the simple beauty of life here, thinking how modern society had divorced itself from the wholesomeness that embodies God's freely given love.

When the purchases were completed we began to make our way through the crowd towards the road, and to the waiting taxies. I decided to take a last look up the hill. As I looked up I saw the sun spinning again. At that moment a woman in traditional black peasant dress began to pass me. I said to her, "Look," as I pointed upward, "the sun is spinning." With a smile of confidence on her face she said, "No have see, believe," pointing to her heart (Jn 20:29).

When we returned, the bus was at the guest house. The driver was loading our luggage. Merissa and the family were out front, waiting to say goodbye. I embraced them, looking for Jozo, who was nowhere to be found. I felt badly about not being able to say goodbye to him, but the cab was waiting to take us to church for our last Mass before leaving.

As I entered the taxi I began to cry. It just came over me. The thought of leaving Medjugorje had begun to set in. It was hard for me to bear. I cried uncontrollably all the way to church and through the better part of Mass. My traveling companions stayed close to me, but allowed me my tears. I felt so comfortable being with them on this trip. The church was packed with people and we had to stand in the isle. I knew that they would understand my sobbing. When you're so close to the love of God, the truth of who we are and what we feel cannot be disguised.

After the Mass I went to the back of the church by the sacristy door and waited to have my religious articles and oil blessed. I sought out the same priest who had heard my confession on my first trip. I had felt drawn to him over the last months, coming to terms with our conversation, and accepting him for who he is, differences notwithstanding.

It was important for me to have these articles blessed only by him. It was as though Our Lady wanted me to reconcile with him, at least in a sense of brotherly love.

After leaving Father I walked towards the bus. Vincent came running towards me and said, "Jozo is here! he came to say goodbye to you!" My eyes started to well up as we looked for him.

When we found him, I hugged him and thanked him while struggling to hold back the tears. As I boarded the bus, that feeling of not wanting to leave overtook me again, and I began to miss the presence of God's love in these wonderful Croation people. The travel brochure was right when it said, "Yugoslavs may seem cold and straight-faced, but do break the ice and you will be surprised." I, for one, am glad I did.

25

Bridging Two Worlds

As we drove away, I knew in my heart that I would return again. The week had passed so quickly. You wouldn't think that a rural place, with no movie theaters, health facilities or boutiques, could keep anyone's interest for more than a couple of hours. There's not even a museum there, let alone a backyard pool. Yet what the Lord provided was so deeply touching. The joy not only lasts a week, but a lifetime.

If asked to describe it, I'd have to say that it's almost like the ancient Hebrew culture. A primitive life, it's similar to what we see depicted in scripture stories. People who live off the land and interact with God and nature. Their houses are of simple stone and masonry construction with no real luxury, yet they live a contented existence. They seem to have consciously and unconsciously accepted the adage of St. Teresa, which says: "God alone suffices." It seems that they have discovered God in their simplicity, where we in our complexity have not only lost sight of Him, but also lost our own identity.

We felt very happy and peaceful as we rode, comparing stories and anticipating our one-day stay in Dubrovnick. After traveling a few hours we stopped at what appeared to be a luxury resort hotel. It sat on an ocean inlet near the Adriatic Sea. We purchased our lunch at a coffee bar inside and sat outside enjoying the view while we ate. I was very relaxed and content, peacefully watching sunbathers and passing boats. The Dubrovnik area is referred to as the Yugoslavian Riviera. Scenic and temperate with a reputation for moderate prices, it's a hot vacation spot for European neighbors, especially Italy, being about a twelve-hour ferry ride across the Adriatic Sea.

It was a nice interlude and quite a contrast to the last time I journeyed home from Medjugorje. We arrived in Dubrovnik early in the afternoon. The sights were breathtaking, as the bus climbed high up the mountain road through the new city. We arrived at our hotel which had a spectacular view of the Adriatic. It seemed to be built into a cliff. This was a special treat for me. The last time I hadn't made it to Dubrovnik so now I had time to spend in the city and take in its beauty.

The old city is authentically medieval with monuments which date back a thousand years. Historically it competed with the renowned Venice as a cultural center and economic power. We were anxious to check in and visit the old city which is noted for its museums and historic buildings.

When we got to the front desk with our luggage, the clerk asked us for our passports. He instructed us to leave them with him for a couple of hours, so he could log them in. As you may have expected my blood pressure began to climb. "No way," I told him, "No way." Gordana tried to reassure me that it would be alright, since I suggested to the others that they shouldn't part with theirs either. I told her the same thing: "No, way. It's not leaving my sight. Don't you remember what happened the last time, Gordana? No way!" She spoke to him in Croation and he nodded his head in understanding. She probably explained to him what had happened to me. He smiled reassuringly, and asked me to wait, while he and another clerk then completed the records.

My room was clean and plain. The hotel accommodations are not luxurious in Yugoslavia. The lighting is kept dim to conserve energy. The building materials they use are durable, but without decor.

When we met in the lobby, Carol, Marie and Vince informed me that they had decided to take a swim so Father Jim, Loraine Luciano and I elected to spend the day visiting the old city together. We all planned to meet later for dinner.

As we took the brisk ten minute walk down to the old city we passed beautiful verandas overlooking the ocean. There were parks pocketed in the side of the mountain, along with commercial buildings and homes, all with breathtaking views of the picturesque shoreline. The sidewalk was narrow, which I understand is typical of European cities, yet it was spotlessly clean and well maintained. As we continued our descent through the main road, Father Jim who had been there before, pointed out various little chapels and historical sights. Most of the buildings were sectioned off with glass partitions, allowing poeple to look through without disturbing the contents.

We finally came to an authentic drawbridge, the main entrance to the ancient city. Looking down as we walked through, I realized how the moat spanned a severe drop. Our priest/tour guide enthusiastically led us through the piazzas and the abundant gift shops. As we browsed through the shops, I began thinking about Joan, wishing that she were with me. She loves to browse and would have enjoyed the diversity of shops and articles.

Her fear of flying frustrated me now, especially after what I had accomplished. I tried to explain to her that Our Lady would give her all the graces she needed to fly, if she would pray. After all, if I could do it, she could do It! She knew how difficult it was for me. This made me realize how important it is for each of us to slay our own dragons. We must turn to God in prayer, ask His help with our frailties, and trust His plan. Because of what I had experienced, I knew that only she could do it. She had to want to grow and find the truth in herself for herself, and that had to be in her own time.

The stone streets were shiny due to centuries of wear and tear. It was a cozy place. The center plazas were small enough to shout across and be heard on the other side. Father took us to more museums and ornate municipal buildings. What I enjoyed most of all was visiting the Church of St. Blaise. Its artwork had the markings of the Renaissance and we were, unexpectedly, able to hear Mass and then purchase candles and medals which were displayed in the old sacristy. The church was small and simple with an ornate altar and tabernacle. You could see that the whole city was not designed for excessive numbers of people. I guess in those days they didn't have a bursting population problem.

St. Blaise the Bishop of Sebastea (Armenia) was martyred around the year 316. He had been born into a wealthy family of noble parents, and became a bishop when he was still quite young. At the time of the Roman persecution of Christians, he fled by divine direction to mountain caves which were inhabited by wild animals. He became noted for healing sick and wounded animals. When he was captured by Roman hunters he was found surrounded by animals, who, tradition has it, came to him for his blessing.

Today he is commonly known as the patron saint of people who suffer from throat disorders. It is said that a woman had brought him a little boy who was near death because a fish-bone had lodged in his throat. The saint had healed him. The church today celebrates his feast day on February 3 with a blessing of throats.

Our competent priest/tour guide did a fantastic job of showing us the city. Taking a short detour, he led us out another drawbridge down by the seashore, to the marina. What a sight, standing there on the dock looking up at the mountain and the walled city, with its backdrop of colorful cliffs. We could see hotels in the distance that were embedded in the hillside. When we looked out to sea we saw beautiful islands surrounded by calm ultramarine blue water. It was breathtaking, to say the least! Our Creator had incredible talent, I thought. Father was eager for us to soak up as much as we could in our short stay there.

When we re-entered the walled city, Loraine decided to walk back to the hotel. She was tired from the pace of the day and wanted to try and call home. Adding to a perfect day Father continued to lead me through a maze of narrow, but charming streets. They were like small alleyways, loaded with shops and outdoor cafes. Eventually we made our way to a cozy sidewalk restaurant and waited for the swimmers.

Marie, Paul Szybillo, Lisa and David Hoebelheinrich arrived soon after. Marie explained that Carol's migraine had returned and that they would rest and have dinner at the hotel. Before dinner we stopped in a few more shops that were close to the restaurant and we made a few quick purchases. Returning to the restaurant we had a great dinner, scampi and all. It was very romantic sitting under umbrellas, watching the table lanterns flicker and brighten as the sky darkened. Topping it all off, Father paid the tab. I really missed Joan and felt sad that she hadn't taken this wonderful trip with me. It felt as though Our Lady had wanted this trip to be perfect for me, a reward for working through the challenges of my last journey.

After dinner, Father again led us through the city and over the drawbridge to the plaza on the main road, where we stopped again to browse at a sidewalk vendor. The walk back was terrific. We could see the panoramic view in the moonlight.

It was late when we got back to the hotel. We met Carol and Vince in the lobby and decided to stop in the lounge for a drink or a cup of coffee and a recounting of our day. The contrast of the time we spent in Medjugorje with that of Dubrovinik that day, gave us a lot of food for conversation. The dialogue was quite lively.

It was remarkable! I thought of how easy it was for us to make the transition from a humble environment, one that based happiness on spiritual revelation, to that of a jet setter, enjoying life's comforts. We talked about the plight of the poor, the welfare system and social issues. It amazed me how conservative some of us were, and the prejudices that still needed to be overcome. When I retired for the evening, I realized how frustrating these social issues are to humanity. People don't feel potent enough to surmount them. The message that comes to me lately is "Do whatever you can." If everyone did something, the problems would be corrected. It reminds me of a saying in the Cursillo movement, "Make a friend, be a friend, bring a friend to Christ!"

When we stopped at the desk for our keys the desk clerk handed us each a bag that contained our breakfast, a ham and cheese sandwich and a piece of fruit. A humbling sign! Gordana's hand written note inside the bag reminded us that we were leaving for the airport at 5 a.m.

As we boarded the bus that morning, I was excited about returning home and seeing Joan. I was hoping that she would be more amenable to venturing on this journey with me in the future. I hate leaving her but I feel compelled to go. It has become a major part of my life.

We arrived at the airport, checked in and passed through customs with ease. The flight to Zurich was pleasant. After all, I had a friend in the cockpit. Marie had identified herself as a Pan Am employee to the pilot, and mentioned that she was a licensed pilot herself (leisure craft). The pilots invited her to fly in the cockpit with them.

I began to see another side of her. When we landed in Zurich, I overheard part of a conversation she was having with the flight crew and I realized how confident she could be. I noted how gifted she was. It's funny how we see ourselves. We seem to zero in on our weaknesses rather than our gifts and in doing so attract people who enjoy pointing out our faults. While we sat on the 747, I mentioned to her what I had observed. I reminded her and myself that we needed to focus on our special God-given qualities and gifts.

It's my guess that many of us live with paradoxical ideas of ourselves. That's why Christian community is so important. It reminds us of our strengths and forgives our weakness as we grow together.

The trip back was super. I was given a seat next to Marie. Carol, Vince and Marie were flying business class and because there was a mix-up on my seat reservation, the flight attendant, with Carol and Marie's coaxing, bumped me up to business class. I'm sure Our Lady's hand was in on this one, too.

After awhile, Vince decided to visit Father Jim and the other pilgrims who were in coach class. When he came back Vince said that Father was mad at me! With his dry sense of humor, Father had told Vince "Sure, look at that Al, our illustrious tour coordinator, riding in comfort, while we sit stuffed here in coach. Tell him, I'm not talking to him." That was Father's way of saying that he missed me. When I went back a few minutes later, I asked Father in Polish to give me a kiss (Daj Mnie Buzi) and reached over to kiss him, while he protested. Vince had taught me how to say, "Give me a kiss" in Polish earlier in the week, just so I could tease Father. Father's immediate reply was, "Get away from me. How do you get to sit up there and we have to stay here?" We talked for awhile and as I left to check the other pilgrims and return to my seat, he said again with a smile on his face, "Sure, go sit in comfort." Father must have had a Sicilian mother.

The flight was perfect for me, just like riding on a magic carpet. Returning home with my pals, thinking about all we had experienced together, I knew in my heart that we'd be lifelong friends. The flight attendants showed us two movies. Since the shades had to be lowered on the windows so that the picture could be viewed clearly, my only regret was that I couldn't look out over the clouds.

26

Conclusion: The Onward Process of Conversion

MEDJUGORJE HAS DEEPLY AFFECTED ME: The experience will last me my lifetime. It healed me, affirmed me, humbled me, and converted me to a life dedicated to God. There is no turning back. I'm over the spiritual hill that I had been trying to climb from the first moment I sought God.

When I returned home after my first trip it was difficult to readjust to the lifestyle there. The second time was just as difficult. My worldly goals aren't as important as they once were. The way I look at things and approach my ministry is changing. My business activity doesn't seem to have the same impact or excitement. It seems that all of the things that make up my value system have been drastically affected.

I can understand now how people who have claimed to have

life-after-death experiences say about the tremendous peace they experienced before they were called back to life. Many of them have claimed that they would never fear death again.

The same kind of feeling now exists within me. After witnessing Our Lady's and Our Lord's presence firsthand, I have a burning desire to return to Medjugorje and place myself again under the umbrella of its heavenly peace.

When I discussed these feelings with my pastor, Father Charlie Papa he related it to the transformation passage in Scripture when Peter, James and John accompanied Jesus up the mountain and they saw Moses and Elijah and heard God's voice (Mk 9:2). They wanted to erect booths. They wanted to stay there in that peaceful place. But Jesus said, in effect, "Let's go back down the hill. We have work to do. You have to deliver the good news."

That's the situation I find myself in now. I know where I want to be, but God has work for me to do. Writing this book may be part of my task. It certainly has been a compulsion. Since my first trip, I have felt driven to share my experiences with my brothers and sisters in every area of my life. It mystifies me how I find the words, having never considered myself adept for professional writing. This account was to be a personal journal, for my own reflection. But as friends and acquaintances read through my notes, they urged me to continue and let the Lord decide its use and success. They further suggested that the finished manuscript be distributed through friends in my spiritual community and ministry.

Miracles never cease! I got a call one day from John Westerman, a professional writer, who happens to live in my condo complex. His call came at a time when I was feeling overwhelmed by this writing. John explained that a mutual friend had mentioned that I had undertaken this writing project and that he was personally interested in the subject matter. Sharing with me that a friend of his had recently given him a book about the apparitions in Fatima, he enthusiastically agreed to read my manuscript. He called about a week later to tell me that he loved the book and that it had touched him deeply. He agreed to meet me for lunch to make suggestions about editing. I was ecstatic. To think that a professional would find merit in my work flabbergasted me. When we met he expressed a strong interest in learning more about Medjugorje. He was so taken by the subject matter that he volunteered to do the editing. I couldn't believe it! Our Lady had done it again! What are the odds of having a published fiction writer as a neighbor? He was even willing to interrupt his own writing (final editing of his fourth book and screenplay) to assist a rank beginner, whom he didn't know. He felt driven.

Thinking back on all the supernatural events that occurred on my trip, I wonder why, out of the millions upon millions of people in the world, I was chosen and blessed to witness firsthand God's mighty presence, to experience the joy and peace of His love. I didn't feel worthy then and I don't feel worthy now.

While watching the television news one evening I saw President Bush commenting to news reporters and thought to myself, "Did he and the other powerful leaders in the world know that Our Lady was appearing?" I realized for the first time that even though I was one of many people who experienced miracles in Medjugorje, we were an infinitesimal percentage of the world population. It boggles the mind when you think of it that way. I ask myself, "Why did He pick me for this? I can think of many people who have not sinned the way I have in life, people who fit the classic holy person stereotype. I don't have the influence that a famous religious, political or theatrical figure would have. Johnny Carson doesn't have me on his television show guest list agenda."

But then I think about the early apostles. These simple unsophisticated men—fisherman, tax collectors, sinners. (Mk 4:18-22) driven by their love for Jesus, had accepted the task of evangelization. Traveling to foreign lands they suffered persecution and hardship just as Our Lord had, yet, with all their failings and human weaknesses, they were chosen to share the good news. The Holy Spirit accomplished great things through them. St. Paul writes, "My grace [the Lord's] is all you need, for my power is greatest when you are weak" (2Cor 12:9). I think of the visionaries. They are average children from a remote European village. They are accomplishing great things for God just as the Apostles did. So, why not me? I just pray that I will be able to live up to this gift that God has bestowed upon me. Knowing full well now that I have a greater responsibility, I pray that I will act according to His will in all that I do.

I feel strongly compelled to faithfully relate Our Lady's message of love and give witness to those I meet, encouraging them to seek God as I did, to convert and to accept His spiritual healing. I want them to experience for themselves the biggest miracle of all, communion with God. I have ceased to fear death. The concept of death for me had always been part of my struggle in faith. I always had difficulty trusting and putting myself in God's hands.

The flying issue epitomizes all the phobias I had that related to the issue of control. The first step of trust was taken when I boarded that 747. The Lord took care of the rest. The world, as we know it, could be likened to one big 747 with God as the pilot.

Through my pilgrimage, He touched those troubled areas inside me, fine tuning, guiding and teaching. He made himself present to me through my prayer experiences. I felt His joyful presence in those people I met along the way.

Our Lady continues to touch my life today. I've grown accustomed to Her miracles. I was feeling disconnected and down a few days after I got back from my initial trip. It seemed that the world was hitting me right between the eyes. Bill collectors, were on the phone. Clients were being difficult about paying what they owed me. As disillusionment began to set in, the doorbell rang. A young man introduced himself as one of those bill collectors. I was very embarrassed. I told him I had expected payment from one of my clients before I went on a trip to Yugoslavia. The client had failed to pay me but I was expecting more receivables momentarily. I reassured him that I had every intention of clearing up the outstanding balance. The young man said, "Yugoslavia! Did you go to that place, Med.. Medju..." "I said, "Medjugorje!" He said, "Yes! that's it!" Reaching under his shirt collar he came up with a gold chain with a gold rosary ring on it. His girlfriend had it blessed for him in Medjugorje.

We wound up sitting on my patio while I related my experiences to him. We finished talking about an hour later he stood up and hugged me. Our Lady was sending me a much needed embrace and affirmation that Medjugorje will continue to happen for me and others through the sharing of faith.

The next week the client who owed me the money met me for lunch. Something told me to bring him a copy of Wiebel's book about Medjugorje. He accepted it with interest. We spent ninety percent of our time at lunch discussing Medjugorje and the necessity of prayer in our life. A week later he agreed to pay me all that he owed. He also told me that he was discussing the phenomena with friends and sharing the book with them. More seeds were being planted.

The same week I was writing the chapter about Cornelia I got a strong feeling to call Jozo in Medjugorje. His daughter told me that he was not home and to call back. Before hanging up I asked her what had happened to Cornelia. She very excitedly explained that Cornelia was presently back in Medjugorje and that she was attending Mass every day and praying the Rosary she exclaimed that Cornelia had been cured!

I remembered approaching Cornelia and her sister the day I left, they were seated on a bench at the side of the church looking at the sunset. Cornelia looked much calmer, with the expression of tired relief, like one looks after a fever breaks. I had reassured her again, as Our Lady had requested, and then said goodbye. I brought back religious medals and rosaries for friends and family. All seemed very touched when they received them. Many, including my mailman, claimed they got the chills when they took them into their hands.

New neighbors moved into a nearby condo unit. They asked about the local church. In the conversation they shared that they hadn't received the Eucharist in over twenty-eight years. They further explained that they felt rejected by the church. One of them had been divorced and was refused absolution, so they weren't married in the church. I suggested that they make an appointment to visit our pastor, and seek reconciliation. I told them of Our Lady's presence in Medjugorje and her message of God's profound love for us. I had purchased a holy water font in Medjugorje while there. I had no one in mind when I bought it. All of a sudden I thought of our new friends and as if inspired I made them a gift of it. Their reaction was one of joy with tears of happiness. I just knew it was Our Lady's wish for them to have it. In a short time, they began to attend Mass. Their adult children have been so inspired by the fire of their conversion, that they have also returned to the Church. One of them even started to volunteer time to a church youth group.

Through the writing of this book there have been many spiritual and emotional healings already. A neighbor of mine, Sylvia, an older lady who lives alone, had also suffered from the effects of church rejection because of a divorce many years before. She generously utilized her God-given gift for grammar to aid me in the editing process. We have developed a close bond through our discussions and work together, and have become family. To sum it up in her words, "I've decided that you need a mother, and I a son."

I can truly see now how Our Lady utilizes and comforts me. I've developed a keener sense for discerning my actions, especially with regard to delivering Her messages. It seems that I've done some bonding of my own.

Speaking of bonding, my daughter Lori gave birth to our first grandchild, Justin and with my proud son-in-law, Rob, we are learning to bond first hand. We had been politely asked to wait awhile before visiting our new grandson when he was brought home so that his parents could insure proper bonding, undisturbed!

Apparently Joan and I were not the only grandparents who were getting a lesson in bonding. While we were waiting in the fathers' lounge for our new arrival, another family, with both sets of prospective grandparents who had been subjected to a twenty-two hour wait, had to wait an additional two and a half hours after their grandchild was born to find out its sex, size and weight. It seems the new parents had to immediately bond with the baby. What ever happened to the proud father informing the family of the new arrival?

The following day I met one of the grandmothers in the waiting room and we laughed about the tension of the night before. She admitted that they all had gotten on each other's nerves the night before. In their minds each blamed the other's child for all the suspense. We chuckled at this bonding business. It was ironic that I had the chapter of the book with me that spoke of bonding. I let her read it. She laughed heartily as she read. When she completed the chapter she claimed that she felt drawn to know more about Medjugorje. I told her that if and when the book was published, I would send her a copy.

Later that afternoon in the same waiting room I met a young Orthodox Jewish man, an expectant father. He was reading a Hebrew prayerbook, while I was reading my moral theology book. Here we were, both coming from two different viewpoints, seeking relationship and understanding of our God. Different in so many ways, we were very similar in our thirst for Him. I told him what I was reading. As our conversation continued I produced a news clipping of an article written about a recent ecumenical conference. It explained how the Catholic Church genuinely accepted some responsibility for creating prejudice against the Jewish faith community over the centuries. As he read the article the young man said he had heard of this, but was cautiously optimistic.

He was very disciplined and committed to a life with God as its center for someone so young. In curiosity I asked him if the traditions of his church (the many laws of the Torah) made him feel confined, especially with all the distractions of modern life? Had he experienced a crossroad or struggle? How did he make the decision to adopt the belief of his parents and ancestors? His answer was sincere and genuine. "This is the life I was born to," he said. "It fulfills me, I feel content and comfortable with it." He reminded me of Jozo, who had the same resolve, one with his God, family and community, "growing where he was planted." They are both living Our Lady's message in their own way, a life committed to God.

I see my environment differently now; people are more special to me. I can see God's love for them and a future of hope. I feel a freedom inside of me, things that I thought were impossible are now achievable. My God today is an ever-present God, committed and involved in my life in an intimate way. My neighbor told me about a picture of Jesus his mother had. It showed Him standing and knocking at a door with no doorknob on His side. I know now that it's up to us to open that door to Him, and I think that's what I did by traveling to Medjugorje. I trusted Him, and He filled me with joy and wonder. He gave me gifts and graces that not only emanate from Medjugorje, but from within me and in my own backyard. His presence is felt wherever I am.

Carol, Vince, Joan and I, visited the Our Lady of the Island Shrine on Long Island. It was the feast of The Holy Rosary. We prayed as we strolled "the rosary walk." Attending an intimate Mass in the chapel, we coincidently met another pilgrim who introduced himself to us, when he heard us singing "Ave Maria" after each decade of the Rosary (a Medjugorje tradition). After we shared our experiences we went to pray at the cross of Calvary and then to a replica of Jesus' Tomb. It is inscribed with the words "Why do you seek Jesus of Nazareth here, He has risen!" As we began to walk away Carol shouted to us "The sun is spinning." Carol, Vince and I thanked the Lord again for his gift as we watched. I thought of the words in Our Lady's favorite song: "... and His truth goes marching on."

> *May the Lord our God bestow upon you his infinite grace, and continue to open your hearts to his unconditional love and lasting peace. Amen.*
>
> *Our Lady Queen Of Peace, pray for us.*

CONSECRATION TO THE HEART OF JESUS

(Dictated to Jelena on November 28, 1983)

O Jesus, we know that you are sweet (Mt11:29).
That You have given Your Heart for us.
It was crowned with thorns by our sins.
We know that today You still pray for us
so that we will not be lost.
Jesus remember us if we fall into sin.
Through Your most Sacred Heart,
make us all love one another.
Cause hatred to disappear among men.
Show us Your Love.
All of us love You.
And we desire that you protect us with Your
Heart of the Good Shepherd.
Enter into each heart, Jesus!
Knock on the door of our Hearts.
Be patient and tenacious with us.
We are still locked up in ourselves, because we
have not understood Your will.
Knock continuously, Oh Jesus
Make our hearts open up to you,
at least when we remember the passion
which you suffered for us. Amen.

CONSECRATION TO THE IMMACULATE HEART OF MARY

(Dictated to Jelena, November 28, 1983)

O Immaculate Heart of Mary, overflowing

with goodness, show us your love for us.

May the flame of your Heart, Oh Mary,

Descend upon all peoples.

We love you immensely.

Impress in our Hearts a true love.

May our hearts yearn for you.

Oh Mary, sweet and humble of heart,

Remember us when we sin.

To know that we men are sinners.

Through your most sacred and maternal heart,

Cure us from every spiritual illness.

Make us capable of looking at the beauty

of your maternal heart,

And that, thus, we may be converted

to the flame of your heart. Amen.

Selected Messages from Our Lady in Medjugorje

October 1981 - " The Russian People will be the people who will glorify God the most. The West has made civilization progress, but without God, as if they were their own creators."

November 6, 1981 - "Do not be afraid! I have shown you Hell so that you may know the state of those who are there."

February 9, 1982 - "Pray for the sick. Believe firmly. I will come to help, according to that which is in my power. I will ask my Son, Jesus, to help them. The most important thing, in the meantime, is a strong faith. Numerous sick persons think that it is sufficient to come here in order to be quickly healed. Some of them do not even believe in God and even less in the apparitions, and then they ask for help from Gospa."

July 12, 1982 - "The third world war will not take place."

July 21, 1982 - "There are many souls in Purgatory. There are also persons who have been consecrated to God - some priests, some religious. Pray for their intentions, at least The Lord's Prayer, the Hail Mary, and the Glory Be seven times each, and the Creed. I recommend it to you. There is a large number of souls who have been in Purgatory for a long time because no one prays for them.

July 24, 1982 - "You go to Heaven in full conscience: that which you have now. At the moment of death, you are conscious of the separation of the body and soul. It is false to teach people that you are reborn many times and that you pass to different bodies. One is born only once. The body, drawn from the earth, decomposes after death. It never comes back to life again. Man receives a transfigured body."

January 10, 1983 - "Men who go to Hell no longer want to receive any benefit from God. They do not repent nor do they cease to revolt and to blaspheme. They make up their mind to live in Hell and do not contemplate leaving it."

January 10, 1983 - "In Purgatory there are different levels; the lowest is close to Hell and the highest gradually draws near to Heaven. It is not on All Soul's Day, but at Christmas, that the greatest number of souls leave Purgatory. There are in Purgatory, souls who pray ardently to God, but for whom no relative or friend pray on earth. God makes them benefit from the prayers of other people. It happens that God permits them to manifest themselves in different ways, close to their relatives on earth, in order to remind men of the existence of Purgatory and to solicit their prayers to come close to God who is just, but good. A small number go directly to Heaven."

March 29, 1984 - "Dear children! In a special way this evening I am calling you to perseverance in trials. Consider how the Almighty is still suffering today on account of your sins. So when suffering comes, offer them up as a sacrifice to God. Thank you for having responded to my call."

July 19, 1984 - "Dear children! These days you have been experiencing how Satan is working. I am always with you, and don't you be afraid of temptations because God is always watching over us. Also I have given myself to you and I sympathize with you even in the smallest temptation. Thank you for having responded to my call."

September 20, 1984 - "Dear children! Today I call on you to begin fasting with the heart. There are many people who are fasting but only because everyone is fasting. It has become a custom which no one wants to stop. I ask the parish to fast out of gratitude because God has allowed me to stay this long in this parish. Dear children fast and prayer with the heart. Thank you for having responded to my call."

October 18, 1984 - "Dear children! Today I call on you to read the Bible every day in your homes and let it be in a visible place so as always to encourage you to read it and to pray. Thank you for having responded to my call."

January 14, 1985 - "My dear children! Satan is so strong and with all his might wants to disturb my plans which I have begun with you. You pray, just pray and don't stop for a minute. I will pray to my Son for the realization of all the plans I have begun. Be patient and constant in your prayers. And don't let Satan discourage you. He is working hard in the world. Be on your guard!"

March 14, 1985 - "Dear children! In your life you have all experienced light and darkness. God grants to every person to recognize good and evil. I am calling you to the light which you should carry to all the people who are in darkness. People who are in darkness daily come into your homes. Dear children, give them the light! Thank you for having responded to my call."

March 24, 1985 - "Today I wish to call you all to confession, even if you have confessed a few days ago. I wish that you all experience my feast day within yourselves. But you cannot experience it unless you abandon yourselves completely to God. Therefore, I am inviting you all to reconciliation with God!"

May 9, 1985 - "Dear children! No you do not know how many graces God is giving you. You do not want to move ahead during these days when the Holy Spirit is working in a special way. Your hearts are turned toward the things of earth and they preoccupy you. Turn your hearts toward prayer and seek the Holy Spirit to be poured out on you. Thank you for having responded to my call.

June 25, 1985 - "I invite you to call on everyone to pray the rosary. With the rosary you shall overcome all the adversities which Satan is trying to inflict on the Catholic Church. All you priests, pray the rosary! Dedicate your time to the rosary!'

November 7, 1985 - "Dear children! I am calling you to love your neighbor and love toward the one from whom evil comes to you. In that way with love you will be able to discern the intentions of hearts. Pray and love, dear children! By love you are able to do even that which you think is impossible. Thank you for having responded to my call."

December 12, 1985 - "Dear children! For Christmas my invitation to you is that on that day we glorify Jesus and His nativity. Dear children, on that day pray still more and think most about Jesus. Thank you for having responded to my call."

April 3, 1986 - "Dear children! I wish to call you to a living of the Holy Mass. There are many of you who have sensed the beauty of the Holy Mass, but there are also those who come unwillingly. I have chosen you, dear children, but Jesus gives you His Graces in the Mass. Therefore, consciously live the Holy Mass and let your coming to it be a joyful one. Come to it with love and make the Mass your own. Thank you for having responded to my call.

September 11, 1986 - "Dear children! For these days while you are joyfully celebrating the cross, I desire that your cross also would be a joy for you. Especially, dear children, pray that you may be able to accept sickness and suffering with love the way Jesus accepted them. Only that way shall I be able with joy to give out to you the graces and healings which Jesus is permitting me. Thank you for having responded to my call."

November 6, 1986 - "Dear children! Today I wish to call you to pray for the souls in purgatory. For every soul prayer and grace is necessary to reach God and the love of God. By doing this, dear children, you obtain new intercessors who will help you in life to realize that all earthly things are not important for you, that only Heaven is that for which it is necessary to strive. Therefore, dear children, pray without ceasing that you may be able to help yourselves and the others to whom your prayers will bring joy. Thank you for having responded to my call."

August 25, 1988 - "Dear children! Today I invite you all to rejoice in the life which God gives you. Little children, rejoice in God the Creator because He has created you so wonderfully. Pray that your life be a joyful thanksgiving, which flows out of your heart like a river of joy. Little children, give thanks unceasingly for all that you possess, for each little gift, which God has given you so that a joyful blessing always comes down from God upon your life. Thank you for having responded to my call."

June 25, 1990 - "Dear children! Today I desire to thank you for all your sacrifices and for all your prayers. I am blessing you with my special motherly blessing. I invite you all to decide for God and from day to day to discover His will in prayer. I desire, dear children, to call all of you to a full conversion so that joy may be in your hearts. I am happy that you are here today in such great numbers. Thank you for having responded to my call."

July 25, 1990 - "Dear children! Today I invite you to peace. I have come here as the Queen of Peace, and I desire to enrich you with my motherly peace, I love you, and I desire to bring all of you to the peace which only God gives and which enriches every heart. I invite you to become carriers and witnesses of my peace to this unpeaceful world. Let peace rule in the world, which is without peace and longs for peace. I bless you with my motherly blessing."

September 25, 1990 - "Dear children! Today I invite you to prayer with the heart, in order that your prayer may be a conversation with God. I desire each of you to dedicate more time to God. Satan is strong and wants to destroy and deceive you in many ways. Therefore, my dear children, pray every day that your lives would be a goodness for yourselves and for all those you meet. I am with you and I am protecting you even though Satan wishes to destroy my plans and hinder the desires which the heavenly Father wants to realize here. Thank you for having responded to my call."

October 25, 1990 - "Dear children! Today I call you to pray in a special way and to offer up sacrifices and good deeds for peace in the world. Satan is strong and, with all his strength, tries to destroy the peace which comes from God. Therefore, dear children, pray in a special way with me for peace. I am with you and desire to help you with my prayers and I desire to guide you on the path of peace. I bless you with my motherly blessing. Do not forget to live the messages of peace. Thank you for responding to my call.

November 25, 1990 - "Dear children! Today I invite you to do works of mercy with love and out of love for me and for your brothers and sisters. All that you do for others, do it with great joy and humility towards God. I am with you and day after day I offer your sacrifices and prayers to God for the salvation of the world. Thank you for having responded to my call."

January 25, 1991 - "Dear children! Today, like before, I invite you to prayer. Your prayer should be a prayer for peace. Satan is strong and wishes not only to destroy human life, but also nature and the planet on which you live. Therefore, dear children, pray that you can protect yourselves through prayer with the blessing of God's peace. God sent me to so that I can help you. If you wish to, grasp for the Rosary. Already the Rosary alone can do miracles in the world and in your lives. I bless you and I stay among you as long as it is God's will. Thank you that you will not betray my presence here and I thank you because your response is serving God and peace. Thank you for having responded to my call!"

February 25, 1991 - "Dear children! Today I invite you to decide for God, because distance from God is the fruit of the lack of peace in your hearts. God is only peace. Therefore, approach Him through your personal prayer and then live peace in your hearts, and in this way peace will flow from your hearts like a river into the whole world. Do not speak about peace, but make peace. I am blessing each of you and each good decision of yours. Thank you for having responded to my call."

March 25, 1991 - "Dear children, again today I invite you to live the passion of Jesus in prayer, and in union with Him. Decide to give more time to God who gave you these days of grace. Therefore, dear children, pray and in a special way renew the love for Jesus in your hearts. I am with you, and I accompany you with my blessing and my prayers. Thank you for having responded to my call!"

April 25, 1991 - "Dear children! Today I invite you all so that your prayer be prayer with the heart. Let each of you find time for prayer, so that in your prayer you discover God, I do not desire you to talk about prayer, but to pray. Let your every day be filled with prayer of gratitude to God for life and all that you have. I do not desire your life to pass by in words, but that you glorify God with deeds. I am with you and I am grateful to God for every moment spent with you. Thank you for having responded to my call."

May 25, 1991 - "Dear children! Today I invite all of you who have heard my message of peace to realize it with seriousness and with love in your life. There are many who think that they are doing a lot by talking about the messages but do not live them. Dear children, I invite you to life and to change all the negative in you, so that it all turns into the positive and life. Dear children, I am with you and desire to help each of you to live, and by living to witness the good news. I am here, dear children, to help you and to lead you to heaven, and in heaven is the joy through which you can already live heaven now. Thank you for having responded to my call."

June 25, 1991 - "Dear children! Today on this great day which you have given me, I desire to bless all of you and to say: these days while I am with you are days of grace. I desire to teach you and to help you walk on the path of holiness. There are many people who do not desire to understand my messages and to accept with seriousness what I am saying. But you I therefore call and ask that by your lives and your daily living you witness my presence. If you pray God will help you discover the true reason for my coming. Therefore, little children, pray and read the sacred scriptures so that through my coming you discover the message in sacred scripture for you. Thank you for responding to my call."

July 25, 1991 - "Dear children! Today I invite you to pray for peace. At this time peace is threatened in a special way, and I am seeking from you to renew fasting and prayer in your families. Dear children, I desire you to grasp the seriousness of the situation and that much of what will happen depends on your prayers, and you are praying a little bit! Dear children, I am with you and I am inviting you to begin to pray and fast seriously as in the first days on my coming. Thank you for having responded to my call."

August 25, 1991 - "Dear children! Today also I invite you to prayer, now as never before when my plan has begun to be realized. Satan is strong and wants to sweep away plans of peace and joy and make you think that my son is not strong in His decisions. Therefore, I call all of you, dear children, to pray and fast still more firmly. I invite you to renunciation for nine days so that with your help everything I wanted to realize through the secrets I began in Fatima may be fulfilled. I call you, dear children, to grasp the importance of my coming and the seriousness of the situation. I want to save all souls and present them to God. Therefore, let us pray that everything I have begun be fully realized. Thank you for having responded to my call."

September 25, 1991 - "Dear children! Today in a special way I invite you all to prayer and renunciation. For now as never before Satan wants to show the world his shameful face by which he wants to seduce as many people as possible onto the way of death and sin. Therefore, dear children, help my immaculate heart to triumph in the sinful world. I beseech all of you to offer prayers and sacrifices for my intentions so I can present them to God for what is most necessary. Forget your desires, dear children, and pray for what God desires and not for what you desire. Thank you for having responded to my call."

Glossary

*For those who do not know about scapulars this is how they came to be. **The Brown Scapular** has a centuries-old origin. In the thirteenth century, the Carmelite Order, under stress and in danger, appealed to their patron saint, Our Blessed Mother. Responding to their call she appeared to its general, St. Simon Stock, and gave him "the Scapular Of Carmel."

In presenting it, she said: "This shall be a privilege for you and all Carmelites, that whoever dies wearing this shall not suffer eternal fire." Centuries later in Fatima on October 13, 1917, Our Lady appeared in the sky, holding up to the world the Brown Scapular of Mt. Carmel in a wordless invitation for us to wear this sign of consecration to her Immaculate Heart.

There is also **"The Green Scapular,"** Jozo had given me one before we left for the railroad station as protection for me on my journey to Zagreb. Our Blessed Mother gave this scapular to a nun, Sister Justine Bisqueyburu, a Daughter of Charity of St. Vincent de Paul. Our Lady instructed her in its use. No investiture is necessary, but it should be blessed by a priest and kept on one's person or in one's room. It is inscribed with the prayer, "Immaculate Heart of Mary, pray for us now and at the hour of our death." The Green Scapular was approved by two popes and has accounted for many conversions and cures.

* **Pastoral formation** is a ministry training program, given by The Pastoral Formation Institute of the Diocese of Rockville Center, Rockville Center, New York. The program offers two years of intensive spiritual and theological formation with an opportunity for a third and fourth year of training for particular ministries and/or the diaconate (preparation for ordination as a Deacon in the Catholic Church).

***Cursillo** *[Kur-see-yo, translated as short course]* is a movement with the primary objective to develop in adult christians a consciousness of their power and mission to become leaders in the work of christian renewal. For further information contact The National Cursillo Center, P.O. Box 210226, Dallas, Texas, 75211.

I – BOOKS:

Bubalo, Fra Janko. *A Thousand Encounters with the Blessed Virgin Mary in Medjugorje.* Friends of Medjugorje: Chicago, IL, 1987. (First published in Croation, 1985).

Bubalo, Fra Janko, with Guy Girard & Armand Girard. Les Editions Pauline: Montreal, Canada, 1988.

Craig, Mary. *The Mystery of the Madonna of Medjugorje: Spark from Heaven.* Ave Maria Press: Notre Dame, IN 46556, 1988.

Hummer, Franz and Jungwirth, Christian. *Medjugorje:* Sveta Vastina: Duvno, 1986.

Kraljevic, Svetozar, OFM. *The Apparitions of Our Lady at Medjugorje.* The Press: Quincy IL, 62301-2699 (formerly Franciscan Herald Press), 1984.

— *Pilgrimage.* Paraclete Press: Orlean, MA 1991

Laurentin, Rene with Ljudevit Rupcic. *Is the Virgin Mary Appearing at Medjugorje?* The Word Among Us Press: Washington, D.C. 1984.

McKenna Briege, OSC with Henry Libersat. *Miracles Do Happen.* Veritas: 1987.

O'Carroll, Michael, CSS. *Medjugorje: Facts, Documents, Theology.* Veritas: 1986.

Patrizia, Lori, *Medjugorje Portfolio of Images.* Alba House: 1990.

Rooney, Lucy, SND, and Faricy, Robert, SJ. *Mary Queen of Peace: Is the Mother of God appearing in Medjugorje?* Alba House: 1984.

— *Medjugorje Unfolds: Mary Speaks to the World.* Fowler Wright/Mercier Press: 1985.

— *Medjugorje Retreat.* Alba House: 1989.

Vlasic, Tomislav and Barbaric, Slavko. *Friends of Medjugorje, Meditations.* Milan, 1985.

— *Open Your Hearts to Mary, Queen of Peace.* Milan, 1985, (Associates, Friends of Medjugorje, P.O. Box 7, Milford, OH 45150).

Barbaric, Slavko Fr. O.F.M. *Pray with the Heart: Medjugorje Manner of Prayer.* Franciscan University Press: Steubenville, OH 43952, 1988.

The Riehle Foundation. *A Man Named Father Jozo.* The Riehle Foundation: P.O. Box 7, Milford, OH, 45150.

Two Friends of Medjugorje. *Words from Heaven.* St. James Publishing Co.: Birmingham, AL, 1990.

A Friend of Medjugorje. (6 booklets)
— *In Front Of The Crucifix With our Lady*
— *A Blessing To Save The World*
— *Medjugorje – The Fulfillment Of All Marian Apparitions*
— *Bishop Zanic – What Went Wrong?*
— *Changing History*
— *Understanding Our Lady's Messages*
 St.James Publishing Co.: Birmingham, AL, 1990.

Father Filip Pavic. *Messages to Our Lady To The Parish Of Medjugorje.* The Parish Office, St James Church: 88266 Medjugorje, Yugoslavia.

Weibel, Wayne. *Medjugorje The Message.* Paraclete Press: Orleans, MA, 1989.

— *Letters from Medjugorje.* Paraclete Press: Orleans, MA, 1991.

Mark Miravalle, S.T.D.. *Medjugorje and The Family.* Franciscan University Press: Steubenville, OH 1991.

— *Heart of the Message of Medjugorje.* Franciscan University Press: Steubenville, OH, 1988.

Jan Connell,. *Queen of The Cosmos.* Paraclete Press: Orleans, MA, 1990.

II – VIDEOS

A Call To Holiness, 1990.

Marian Apparitions of the Twentieth Century, 1991

Medjugorje — Sign Transforming Your Heart, 1989
  Marian Videos, Lima, PA.

The Madonna Of Medjugorje, BBC.

Miracles in Medjugorje, 1986.

Love's Call to Freedom, 1988.
  Distributed by Franciscan University of Steubenville, OH.

The Road Home, Living His Life Abundantly, Clearwater, FL, 1988.

Medjugorge — The Lasting Sign, with Martin Sheen, Caritas, 1990.

The Message of Medjugorje, Wayne Weibel, Weibel Columns, Myrtle Beach, S.C.

III – MEDJUGORGE INFORMATION AND PILGRAMAGE CENTERS

Ave Marie Retreat Home
Rt. 1 Box 0368AB
Marrero, LA 70072

Center for Queen of Peace
P.O. Box 90035
Pasadena, CA 91109-0035

Center for Peace
11 Ellsworth Lane
St. Louis, MO 63124

St.Bernardine Catholic Chapel Bookstore
505 S. Flower St.
Arco Plaza, Level C
Los Angeles, CA 90071

Center For Peace - West
5610 Quince St. N.E.
Salem, OR 97305

Ave Maria Center
1405 10th St.
International Falls, MN 56649

Caritas of Birmingham
Box 120-4647
Highway 280 East
Birmingham, AL 35243

International Marian Center
77 Wallace Ave.
Auburn, MA 01501

Center for Peace for No. NJ
P.O. Box 752
North Arlington, NJ 07031

Center for Peace West
P.O.Box 55748
Seattle, WA 98155

Center/Peace-Mossyrock
395 Mossyrock Rd. W.
Mossyrock, WA 98564

Medj. Information Resources
P.O.Box 11938
Albuguerque, NM 87192-0938

Ave Maria Center for Peace
P.O. Box 489 Ste. U
Toronto, Ontario
Canada M8Z 5Y8

Marian Center for Peace
Idaho - P.O. Box 2970
Halley, ID 83333

Medjugorje Info. Center
Box 36, 99 Falcon Crest Dr.
Greenville, SC 29607

Queen of Peace Medj. Center
1055 Charnelton, St.
Eugene, OR 97401

Center for Peace West
5100 S.W. Mac Adam Av.#250
Portland, OR 97201

Children of Mary
3023 W. 84th Terr.
Leawood, KS 66206

Florida's Marian Center/Peace
5700 Fourth St. No.
Suite C
St. Petersburg, FL 33703

Twin Circle Publishing Co.
12700 Ventura Blvd.Su.200
Studio City, CA 91604

Queen of Peace Center of Video Ministries
P.O. Box 8253
Bangor, ME 04402

101 Foundation Inc.
Dr. Rosalie A. Turton
P.O. Box 151

Gospa USA.
Marian Peace Ministry
3700 Oakview Terr. N.E.
Washington, DC 20017

Marion Office of Contemporary Apparitions
Franciscan Univ.of Steubenville
23 Franciscan Way
Steubenville,OH 43952

Living Life Abundantly
702 Bayview Ave.
Clearwater, FL 34619

Fr. Slavko Soldo
502 W. 41st St.
New York, NY 10036

Queen of Peace Center
5706 Trail Meadow Dr.
Dallas, TX 75230

Marian Center
3065 Floyd Blvd.
Sioux City, IA 51105

Marian Medj. Min.
300 Newbury Street
Boston, MA 02115-2805

Mary Immaculate Queen
P.O. Box 16365
Rocky River, OH 44116

Mary`s Messengers Inc.
64 S. Flegg St.
Worcester, MA 01602

Medjugorje Info. Center
P.O.Box 23351
Harahan, LA 70183

Queen of Peace Center
6619 Old Dobbin Drive
Mobile, AL 36695

Mary Immaculate Queen
1177 So. Grace St.
Lombard, IL 60148

Medj., A Message of Peace
340 Prussian Lane
Wayne, PA 19087

Medjugorje Message Center
50 Tynemouth Road
London N15 4AX England

Marian Center
313 East Monroe
Springfield, IL 62701

Mary's Media Foundation
P.O. Box 433
Rye, NY 10580

Medjugorje Messengers
P.O. Box 647
Framingham, MA 01701

Center for Peace
P.O. Box 1425
Concord, MA 01742

Cross of Peace
201 Knight Lane
Santa Maria, CA 93454

Medjugorje Ct.- Las Vegas
4549 E. Harmon Ave.
Las Vegas, NV 89121

Medjugorje Center
7622 Wornall Rd.
Kansas City, MO 64114

Medjugorje Information Service
85 Ridgeview Dr.
Pleasantville, NY 10570

Medjugorje MIR Center
8629 W. Central, Suite 3
Wichita, KS 67212

Medjugorje Star
2627 David Drive
Metaire, LA 70003

Medjugorje Center
31 Cardinal Dr.
Poughkeepsi, NY 12601

Medjugorje Center
3712 N. 92 St.
Milwaukee, WI 53222

Medj. Information Center
7033 Oakes Road
Brecksville, OH 44141

Queen of Peace Center
745 Velma
Memphis, TN 38104

Medjugorje Magazine
P.O. Box 99
Bloomingdale, IL 60108

Medjugorje Network
1140 Ivy Lane
Indianapolis, IN 46220

Medjugorje Witness
P.O. Box 4500 #263
Bloomington, IN 47402

Medjugorje Center
P.O. Box 42
Scott Depot, WV 25560

MIR Center of San Francisco
P.O. Box 6510
San Francisco, CA 94101- 6510

Medjugorje Center
1450 S. 25th St.
Fargo, ND 58103

Medj. Info. Center Erie
P.O. Box 3204
Erie, PA 16508

MIR Center of San Jose
12900 Saratoga-
Sunnyvale Rd.
Saratoga, CA 95070

Medjugorje Message Center
126 E. Washington St.
Chagin Falls, OH 44042

Medjugorje Society
3328 Glenmore Dr.
Falls Church, VA 22041

MIR Group
400 Poydras St.#2650
New Orleans, LA 70130

Chicago Medjugorje Center
1847 West Estes
Chicago, IL 60626

Medj. Ventures
11486 Last Dollar Pass
Littleton, CO 80127

MIR Center of Arizona
P.O. Box 14032
Scottsdale, AZ 85267-4032

Spokane Center for Peace
8601 N. Division Suite D
Spokane, WA 99208

Marian Resource Center
6111 Steubenville, Pike
McKees Rocks, PA 15136

Bellweather Queen of Peace
4014 North Post Rd.
Omaha, NE 68112

Miracle of Medjugorje
8 Booth Rd.
Enfield, CT 06082

Our Lady Queen of Peace Prayer Group
P.O. Box 7556
Garden City, NY 11530

Our Lady's Center
3301 S. Rogers Ave
Ellicott, MD 21043

Pax Regina
7128 Bristol Blvd.
Edina, MN 55435

Pilgrim for Peace Center
5 E. Walnut Ave.
Westmont, NJ 08108

Hearts for Peace
11905 Taylorcrest
Houston, TX 77024

Gospa Missions10106
Kimblewick
Louisville, KY 40223

Riehle Foundation
P.O. Box 7
Milford, OH 45150

Theotokos Apostolate
2530 Secor Road
Toledo, OH 43606

Western N.Y. Center/Peace
P.O. Box 923
Williamsville, NY 14221

Center for Peace - Denver
1934 Forest Parkway
Denver, CO 80220

Queen of Peace Ministries
P.O. Box 761
Notre Dame, IN 46556

Signs of the times
2 Pidgeon Hill Drive Su.280
Sterling VA 22170

Jesus Through Mary Foundation
Rte. 2, Box 110-D
Howe, TX 75059

Queen of Peace Centre
21248 Robinston St.
Regina, Saskatchewan
Canada, S4P 2P7

Queen of Peace Center
9759-47th Ave.
Edmonton Alberta
Canada T6E5M7

Marian Communication, Ltd.
P.O. Box 8
Lima, PA 19037

Mary-Peter Publications
P.O. Box 3620
So. Bend, IN 46619-6620

Our Lady's Center for Peace
1408 So. Second St.
Louisville, KY 40208

Cilento Productions
1409 E. Capitol Drive
Milwaukee, WI 53211-1997

Franciscan University Press
Franciscan Way
Steubenville, OH 43952

Center for Peace
124 1/2 Cass Ave.
Traverse City, MI 49684

Follow Me Communications
18600 Main St, Su. 210
Huntington Beach, CA 92648

Queen of Peace Medj. Center
2121 McFadden Ave.
Beaumont, TX 77701

MIR Peace Translation Center
P.O. Box 105
Clark Summit, PA 18411

Tennessee Center for Peace
1909 West End Ave.
Nashville, TN 37203

Mary's Newsroom
P.O. Box 15455
Pittsburgh, PA 15237

Trinlkria Press
P.O. Box 71283
New Orleans, LA 70172

Dubuque Medj. Center
5071 Asbury Rd.
Dubuque, IA 52001

Medj. Center - St. Charles
2657 Hughway P
Wentzville, MO 63385

Send Your Spirit-Medj.Cen.
P.O. Box 611
Reading, MA 01867

Heart of Medj. Center
2135 Waverly Drive
Anaheim, CA 92802

Pilgrims of Faith
129 Deerfield Ave.
Atco, NJ 08004-2716

Center for Peace
2637 S. King Rd.
Virginis Beach, VA 23452

Morning Star Christian Supply
370 S.W. 17th St.
Boca Raton, FL 33432

Medjugorje Message Center
P.O. Box 97
No. White Plains, NY
10603-0097

Messengers of the Queen of Peace
1309 Crystal Beach Road
Earleville, MD 21919

Uniontown Center for Peace
P.O. Box 812
Uniontown, PA 15401

Weible Columns Medj. Cen.
P.O. Box 2647
Myrtle Beach, SC 29578

Pittsburgh Center for Peace
6111 Steubenville Pike
McKees Rocks, PA 15136

Racine Area Medj. Center
9500 Durand Ave.
Sturtvant, WI 53177

The Medulink Foundation
P/O/Box 25443
Washington, DC 20007

Medjugorje Information & Resource Center
3298 Lake Elouise Loop Rd.
Winter Haven, FL 33884

Oblates of Mary Immaculate
Immaculata Retreat House
P.O.Box 55
289 Windham Rd.
Williamantic, CT 06226-0055

Whitefish Center for Peace
711 Spokane,Ave.
Whitefish, MT 59937

Willene's Religious Joy
921 Main St.
Highland, Il 62249

Queen of Mercy Center
P.O. Box 683
Earth, TX 79031

Medjugorje Center for Love
Suite 362, P.O. Box 5118
Fremont, CA 94537

The Aposolate of the Queen of Peace
P.O.Box 5548
Burlington, VT 05401

Come Alive Communications
P.O. Box 1224
Linwood, PA 19061

The Marian Center
P.O.Box 4240
Pensacola, FL 32507

Medjugorje Center
14955 W. Cleveland Ave.
New Berlin, WI 5315

Florida Center for Peace
P.O. Box 431306
Miami, FL 33143

Marianist House Of Intercession
734 N. 33rd Street
East St.Louis, IL 62205

Mir-A Call Center
3089 C Clairemont Dr.
Suite 331
San Diego, CA 92117

Gospa USA, Inc.-Florida
34 Westmill Lane
Palm Coast, FL 32137

Friends of Medjugorje
300 N. Reagan St.
P.O. Box 527, Suite D
West, TX 76691

Medjugorje Center for Peace-Puerto Rico
34 Barbosa Street,
P.O. Box 748
Isabela, PR 00662

Regina Caell
2729 Salzedo
Coral Gables, FL 33134

Pension For Peace
Box 101
Trempealeau, WI 54661

Our Lady of Unity Apostolate
P.O.Box 56
St. Francis, ME 04774

Center for Peace/North N.J.
P.O.Box 752
North Arlington, NJ 07031

Immaculate Conception Center & Our Lady of the Island Shrine
665 Motts Cove Road North
Roslyn Harbor, NY 11576

Respond Ministry
P.O.Box 7710
Des Moines, IA 50322

A Pilgrims Journey
38 Winter St.
Lynbrook, NY 11563

Medjugorje Resource Center
480 East 6400 South
No. 204-A
Salt Lake City, Utah 84107

Medjugorje Network Of Delaware
P.O. Box 564
Claymont, DE 19703

Friends of Medjugorje
511 Southwood Lane
St. Joseph, MO 64506

Our Mother Queen of Peace Coalition
P.O. Box 117
Glenwood Landing,. NY 11547

Center for Peace
P.O. Box 2206
Marietta, GA 30061

Association Of Marian Helpers
Eden Hill
Stockbridge, MA 01263

Medj. Mary's Invitation To Peace
3206 Lauraine Circle
Santa Fe, NM 87505

Pilgrims Peace Center
410 North Highland Ave.
Clearwater, FL 34615

Dear Children, I invite you to individual conversion. This time is for you. Without you the Lord cannot accomplish what He wants. Dear children, grow every day in prayer, always towards God. I am giving you a weapon against your Goliath. Here are five stones: 1) Pray the Rosary with your heart, 2) Eucharist, 3) Read the Bible, 4) Fasting, 5) Monthly confession.

Photo by Adam Leskowicz. Reproduced with permission.

33. Our Lady's statue in Father Jozo's Church in Tihaljina similar to the one he gives to visiting pilgrims. Note inscription on opposite page.